Keyboard Interpretation

Jack Watson
June 1985
from Eleanor Weber

Keyboard Interpretation

from the 14th to the 19th century

AN INTRODUCTION

HOWARD FERGUSON

NEW YORK & LONDON

Oxford University Press

1975

Library of Congress Catalog Card Number 75–4207

© Oxford University Press 1975

Printed in the United States of America

Contents

Preface

'This book gathers together and considerably expands all the information concerning keyboard instruments, their music, and its interpretation, that first appeared in the introductions to the various anthologies I have edited for the Oxford University Press during the past decade (see page ix). The new format has been planned to allow a clearer presentation of the material, and to obviate the duplications and cross-references that were unavoidable in the earlier volumes.

As before, the main concern is with the stringed keyboard instruments and their music. This does not entirely exclude the organ, however, for before the introduction of organ pedal-boards composers made little stylistic distinction between one keyboard instrument and another, and much of the repertory was common to all. But problems involved with music intended exclusively for the organ are not discussed.

It should be stressed that the book is intended as no more than an introduction to a vast, fascinating, and ever-changing subject. Thus the treatment is selective rather than comprehensive, and more space is devoted to what is for convenience called the Pre-Classical period (roughly prior to 1750) than to either the Classical (*c.* 1750–1830) or the Romantic (*c.* 1830–1900).

The list of Contents (p. v) shows the overall plan of the book, while the detailed Index (pp. 199 ff.) will enable a particular topic to be located. Suggestions for further reading can be found on pp. 177 ff., and some useful modern editions on pp. 180 ff., the latter being grouped under the headings of facsimiles, anthologies, and works by individual composers. Most of the pieces discussed in the book can be found in one or other of my own anthologies.

The following firms have kindly given permission for the quotation or use of copyright material: Hutchinsons Ltd. for the quotation on p. 153 from the late Thurston Dart's *The Interpretation of Music*, 1954; and Penguin Books Ltd. for the use of material from my contribution to the symposium *Keyboard Music*, 1972, edited by Denis Matthews.

Many friends have at one time or another read parts of this book and made valuable suggestions for which I am most grateful. In particular I would like to thank Derek Adlam, Hugh Cobbe, Professor Gerald Hendrie, Christopher Hogwood, Geraint Jones, Professor Denis Matthews, Yfrah Neaman, Alan Ridout, Colin Tilney, and Dr Arnold van Wyk. Dr H. Diack Johnstone kindly allowed me some years ago to read his stimulating but unpublished paper on the ornamentation of English keyboard music; he must not be held responsible for my views, however, for I know he disagrees with some of them.

Finally, I cannot close without recording my great indebtedness to the late Professor Thurston Dart, who gave such invaluable practical help and encouragement during the preparation of the various anthologies on which the book is based.

Howard Ferguson
Stellenbosch and London
1971–2

ABBREVIATIONS USED

CE   Modern complete edition, as listed on pp. 180 ff.

CEKM *Corpus of Early Keyboard Music*, published by the American Institute of Musicology.

EEKM *Early English Keyboard Music*, I–II, ed. Howard Ferguson; Oxford University Press, London 1971.

EFKM *Early French Keyboard Music*, I–II, ed. Howard Ferguson; Oxford University Press, London 1966.

EGKM *Early German Keyboard Music*, I–II, ed. Howard Ferguson; Oxford University Press, London 1970.

EIKM *Early Italian Keyboard Music*, I–II, ed. Howard Ferguson; Oxford University Press, London 1968.

FWVB *The Fitzwilliam Virginal Book*, I–II, ed. W. Barclay Squire and J. A. Fuller Maitland; Breitkopf & Härtel, Leipzig 1899.

MB   *The Mulliner Book*, ed. Denis Stevens; *Musica Britannica*, 1, Stainer & Bell, London 1954 (2nd ed.).

S&I   *Style and Interpretation*, I–IV, ed. Howard Ferguson; Oxford University Press, London 1963–4.

Pitch Notation

1 The Instruments

The keyboard instruments with whose music this book is concerned may be divided into two main groups. In the first group the sounds are produced by air-pressure acting on pipes which may or may not incorporate reeds: i.e. the Church Organ, and smaller organs such as the Positive, Portative, and Regal. In the second group the sounds are produced by strings which are either struck or plucked: i.e. the Echiquier (about which little is known), the Clavichord, the Harpsichord with its smaller relatives the Virginals and Spinet, and the Forte-piano with its descendant the modern Piano.

ORGAN

Of all these instruments, the organ has by far the longest history. It probably originated somewhere in the Middle East; and certainly the Hydraulis, or Water Organ, was known to the Greeks of the 3rd century B.C. and later to the Romans. Early descriptions, and a small clay model of c. A.D. 200 dug up in Carthage, show that in its most developed form the hydraulis had keys, stops, and several ranks of pipes, that the wind was supplied by hand pumps, and the wind pressure stabilized by means of water.

With the fall of the Roman Empire the traditions and skills of organ-building were temporarily lost to Europe; but by the 8th century they had been revived, though lacking many of the refinements that had already been achieved in the hydraulis. Some of the larger medieval organs were crude and powerful. An instrument installed in Winchester in the late 10th century had 400 pipes, two 'manuals' of 20 notes each, and 26 pairs of bellows worked by 'seventy strong men'. It was controlled by two players operating sliders—not keys—each of which opened ten pipes simultaneously. As the latter were presumably of different sizes, and therefore of different pitches, the sound produced must have been formidable. Indeed, it is hard to imagine how it could have been accommodated in the service of the Church.

The more refined instruments that gradually evolved were better suited to their main function of accompanying the liturgy. During the 13th century the cumbersome sliders were replaced by more easily manageable keys; and a century later the chromatic notes F sharp, C sharp, E flat, and G sharp were added one by one to B flat, which originally was the only 'black' note available. By the 15th century multiple keyboards, various types of pipes, and improved mechanism provided a considerable tonal and dynamic range; and there were even short, non-chromatic pedal boards, which at first were attached to the lower manual by lengths of cord, but were later provided with pipes of their own.

In Northern Germany, where the principal developments in organ-building took place, the basic Church Organ had emerged by the beginning of the 16th century. From Arnolt Schlick's *Spiegel der Orgelmacher und Organisten*, 1511, it is apparent that a typical instrument might have consisted of two manuals with a total of fifteen stops, plus an independent pedal department with four stops. A century later Michael Praetorius in his *Syntagma musicum*, 1615, described virtually the type of Baroque organ on which Bach and his contemporaries would have played. One such instrument, in the Peterskirche, Hamburg, had three manuals with a total of thirty-one stops, and a pedal department with no less than ten stops.

Similar organs were built in the Netherlands, France, and Spain; but in Southern Germany, Italy, and England instruments remained smaller and pedal-boards were either primitive or non-existent. (In England pedals were not introduced until 1720, and were even then unpopular with the majority of players.) In cathedrals and larger churches, however, there were often several organs of different sizes. Durham Cathedral, for example, possessed five by the end of the 16th century: the main organ placed above the entrance to the Choir, and four smaller ones dotted here and there for use on different liturgical occasions.

Later developments in organ-building need not here concern us, since the repertory of the 19th-century Romantic type of instrument lies outside the scope of this book.

POSITIVE

The smaller type of organ mentioned above in connection with Durham Cathedral was already in use by the 13th century and was known as a Positive.

An illumination in the Belvoir Psalter of *c.* 1270 shows a player seated at a single-manual instrument which is equipped with keys (not sliders) and a couple of ranks of pipes. The wind is supplied by two bellows worked by the feet of an assistant, who holds on to a horizontal bar for support. Later illustrations show the bellows being worked either by hand or by one of the player's own feet. Such medium-sized instruments, standing either on the ground or on a table, were widely popular, for they could be made large enough for an ecclesiastical establishment, where they would be used during the liturgy, or small enough for a luxurious home, where they could provide both sacred and secular music. Their descendant was the type of 18th-century Chamber Organ that can still be found tucked away in some English churches and cathedrals. Generally it will possess a single manual, half a dozen stops, and bellows that were originally operated by the foot.

PORTATIVE

Smaller still was the Portative (Italian: *organetto*), which could be carried by the player. It had one or two ranks of 'flue' (flute) pipes with a compass of about two octaves, and was played by the right hand alone while the left hand worked the single bellows at the back. When supported by a band slung round the player's neck it could be used in procession; otherwise it was placed on a table or held on the knee. It remained in use, mainly for melodic purposes, from the 12th to the 15th century.

REGAL

The Regal was also small enough to be set on a table, though sometimes it was provided with legs of its own. Originally it consisted entirely of reed stops, which were sufficiently powerful to support a group of singers or instruments such as shawms and sackbuts (the precursors of oboes and trombones). It remained in use from the mid-15th century until well on in the 17th. The so-called Bible Regal, developed in the mid-16th century, was a small version of the instrument that could be folded up like a book.

ECHIQUIER

The history of stringed keyboard instruments is shorter than that of the organ, and little is known of what appears to have been one of the earliest of them all, the Echiquier or Exaquier. It is mentioned in two poems by Guillaume de Machaut (d. 1377), who refers to it as the *échiquier d'Angleterre*, so it may have originated in England. Certainly Edward III gave one in 1360 to John II of France, who was then his captive in the Palace of the Savoy in London. And in 1388 the Spanish king, John I of Aragon, wrote to Philip the Bold, Duke of Burgundy, asking for an experienced player on the *exaquier*, which he said was 'like an organ, but sounding with strings'. A description of what may possibly have been the instrument is found in a manuscript (Paris, Bib. Nat. MS. Latin 7295) written by Henri Arnault of Zwolle (d. 1466), physician to a later Duke of Burgundy. Though the language is none too clear, it would appear that the far end of each key supported a small upright piece of wood with a metal button fixed on top. When the key was struck its travel was limited abruptly by a stop, thus catapulting the small piece of wood upwards, so that the metal button hit the string and produced the note required. The piece of wood, which incorporated a small lead weight, then fell back to its original position on the far end of the key. There is no mention of any dampers.

The interesting point about such an instrument, whether or not it was the *echiquier*, is that its action anticipated the free-flying hammer of the piano, and thus differed basically from that of either the clavichord or the harpsichord (see below). Its tone, too, would have been altogether different, for it must have resembled that of a Hungarian cimbalom when played without the dampers.

Arnault of Zwolle also described the clavichord and harpsichord, both of which were mentioned still earlier by Eberhardt Cersne in *Der Minne Regel*, 1404.

CLAVICHORD

The Clavichord (French: *clavichorde*; German: *Klavichord*; Italian, *clavicordo*, *manicordo*) is in some ways the most perfect of all keyboard instruments. It is oblong in shape, with the keyboard set in one of the long sides and the strings stretching from left to right of the player. The action is extremely simple. At the far end of each key is a small brass blade, or tangent. When the key is depressed the tangent rises and strikes a pair of unison strings, at the same time stopping them like the finger of a violinist's left hand. The section of strings to the right of the tangent vibrates to produce the note required, while the section to the left is damped by a piece of felt wound round the end of the strings. When the key is released the tangent falls back, the whole length of the two strings is damped by the felt, and the note ceases to sound. There is no sustaining pedal.

In early models there was not a separate pair of strings for each key. Instead, the tangents of two or three neighbouring keys struck a single pair of strings at different points—a system which was only practical so long as adjacent semi-tones or tones were unlikely to be required simultaneously. This type of clavichord was known as 'fretted' (German: *gebunden*). In the later 'unfretted' (*bundfrei*) models each key was provided with a pair of strings of its own, and occasionally (to increase the tone) with a third string at 4' pitch for the bass register.

Though the action is so simple it can produce extremely subtle effects; for the clavichordist, unlike the player of any other keyboard instrument, remains in direct (though diminishing) control of the string for as long as the key is depressed. He can therefore produce not only sensitive tonal and dynamic gradations, but also (by means of a slight up-and-down movement of the finger) a very expressive vibrato (German: *Bebung*).

Against this unique sensitiveness must be set the clavichord's lack of power. Its tone is so delicate that it would scarcely be heard in most concert halls; and in ensemble music it cannot stand up to other instruments, or even a single voice. Thus it is essentially a solo or practice instrument for use in the home. In such surroundings its expressiveness is as notable as its unexpected ability to suggest a wide range of dynamics.

The earliest surviving clavichord was made in Italy in 1543. There is little doubt, however, that the instrument existed considerably earlier than even Eberhardt Cersne's reference of 1404. Though its popularity began to wane in England, France, and the Netherlands towards the end of the 16th century, it remained in use until the early 19th century in Italy, Spain, and Germany, largely as a practice instrument for organists, and sometimes with a separate pedal-board attached.

HARPSICHORD, VIRGINALS, AND SPINET

The essential difference between, on the one hand, the clavichord, and, on the other, the Harpsichord, Virginals, and Spinet (French: *clavecin*, *épinette*; German: *Klavicimbel*, *Clavicembalo*, *Spinett*; Italian: *clavicembalo*, *gravicembalo*, *spinetta*) is that the strings of all the latter are plucked by quill or leather plectra instead of being struck by brass tangents. Furthermore, the basic mechanism of even the simplest type of harpsichord is much more complicated than that of the clavichord.

Today the three names stand for three different, though closely related, instruments; but in 16th- and early 17th-century England the word 'virginals' was often used to describe them all. In appearance, the harpsichord resembles a narrow grand piano, the virginals are oblong (or in Italy polygonal), and the spinet is a wing-shaped polygon. The strings of the harpsichord stretch away from the player, as on a grand piano, while those of the virginals and spinet run from left to right, as on the clavichord.

In each instrument the far end of every key supports a slim upright piece of wood called a 'jack', the top of which is level with the strings. (The harpsichord may have more than a single jack for each key, as will be seen later.) Projecting from the side of the jack, and normally resting below the strings, is a plectrum of quill or leather. When the key is depressed the jack and plectrum rise, the latter plucks the string in passing, and the whole string-length vibrates to produce the note required. When the key is released the jack falls back to its original position (an ingenious device allowing the plectrum to pass the string silently), the string is damped by a small piece of felt attached to the upper part of the jack, and the note ceases to sound. Again, there is no sustaining pedal.

Such a plucking action gives a much louder and more brilliant sound than that produced by the tangent of a clavichord; but it cannot provide either continuously variable dynamics or a vibrato. Instead, it relies on less immediately apparent effects such as the smaller tonal differences produced by variations in touch and attack, the expressive potential of notes minutely displaced in the metrical scheme, and the masking of attack on a note by slightly holding over a previous one. Broader tonal contrasts are not available on either the virginals or spinet, for each has only a single manual and one set of strings and jacks. The harpsichord, on the other hand, generally has several sets of strings and jacks, and often more than one manual. (Two manuals tuned a 4th apart were originally used to simplify a frequently required transposition.) Hand-stops or pedals, the latter introduced about 1675, enable the player to use whichever set of strings, or combination of sets, he may require. He can thus produce a limited number of tonal and dynamic contrasts—but not a gradual crescendo or diminuendo, since the changes must always be made in clearly defined steps.

A surviving English harpsichord of 1755 has the following specification:

2 keyboards of five octaves each.

3 sets of strings: one of 8-foot pitch and one of 4-foot pitch (that is, sounding an octave higher than written) activated from the lower keyboard; and a second, contrasting set of strings of 8-foot pitch worked from both keyboards. This contrasting 8-foot register is provided with a second set of jacks, placed closer to the ends of the strings, which are worked from the top keyboard only and produce a sound like a lute.

4 hand-stops: one for each 8-foot and 4-foot register of the lower keyboard; one for the contrasting 8-foot register operated by both keyboards; and one for the lute effect on the top keyboard.

With these resources a considerable range of dynamics and tone-colours can be produced—though only, as already pointed out, in distinct steps. Furthermore, if these involve a change of hand-stops, and not merely a shift from one manual to the other, they will always take an appreciable time to effect. Modern instruments with pedals instead of stops can make changes of registration without this break. There is no indication, however, that any of the great harpsichord composers ever used such a device or relied on it for the performance of their music.

The single register of the spinet is clear and brilliant, while that of the virginals depends on the position of the keyboard. When the latter is to the left of centre (this model is known as a *spinette*) the tone is similar to a spinet's; when it is to the right (a *muselar*) the sound is rounder and more mellow, for the plucking-point is nearer to the centre of the strings.

The earliest surviving harpsichord was made in Italy in 1521. But Henri Arnault's manuscript describes a still earlier version of the instrument, and another appears in an illumination of the Duc de Berry's *Très belles heures*, of *c.* 1416. Both the harpsichord and the spinet remained popular throughout Europe until they were finally superseded about 1780 by the more 'expressive' and equally powerful fortepiano (see below). The virginals were confined mainly to the Netherlands and England, and became outmoded towards the end of the 17th century. Harpsichords (like clavichords) sometimes had separate pedal-boards to enable organists to practise at home.

SHORT OCTAVE TUNING

On all of these instruments, including the organ, the downward compass was sometimes extended, without increasing the length of the keyboard, by means of either Short Octave Tuning, or a constructional device known as the Broken Octave. The two methods were related and worked as follows. On a keyboard that apparently ended with the bass note E, this key in fact sounded the C a 3rd lower. The resulting gap was filled diatonically by tuning the nearby F-sharp and G-sharp keys to D and E respectively. (See Ex. 1a, below, where the altered notes are shown in bold type.) Similarly, a keyboard apparently ending with the bass note B_1 could be extended a 3rd lower to G_1 (see Ex. 1b). The downward compass of each instrument was thus increased by a 3rd, at the cost of only two rarely required chromatic notes. When the absence of the latter became musically inconvenient (towards the end of the 16th century) it was found possible to restore them by the use of the 'broken octave'. The black keys concerned were split in two, so that the front half of each would produce its 'short octave' diatonic note, while the back half played the normal chromatic note (see Exx. 1c and 1d).

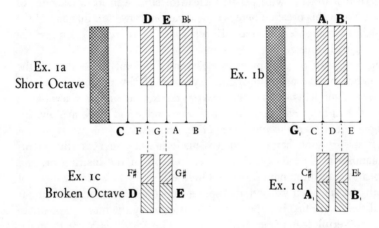

Ex. 1a
Short Octave

Ex. 1b

Ex. 1c
Broken Octave

Ex. 1d

These methods of tuning account for certain apparently unplayable bass chords that are occasionally found in virginals music. For example, Peter Philips writes the following l.h. passage in his 'Pavana Dolorosa', *Fitzwilliam Virginal Book* (hereafter called *FWVB*) I, p. 321:

Ex. 2

Few players could manage this with one hand on a normal keyboard; yet with the tunings shown in either Exx. 1a or 1c it would involve no more than the following easy stretches:

Ex. 3

FORTEPIANO AND PIANOFORTE

In discussing the most recent pair of stringed keyboard instruments it will be convenient to use the words Fortepiano and Pianoforte to distinguish between, respectively, the early type of piano and its modern descendant. The distinction is important, for there is as great a difference of tone, and almost as great a difference of touch, between an early fortepiano and a modern pianoforte as there is between a fortepiano and either a harpsichord or a clavichord. Thus defined, a fortepiano has a mainly wooden frame, thin, comparatively low-tensioned strings, and small leather-covered hammers; while a pianoforte has an iron frame, thicker, high-tensioned strings, and larger felt-covered hammers.

In appearance the fortepiano resembled either a harpsichord, with the strings stretching away from the player, or a large clavichord, with strings stretching from left to right. The first type was known as a 'grand' and the second as a 'square' piano. Later, with the introduction of iron frames and longer keyboards, the slim and elegant shape of the early grand turned into the broader, heavier-looking instrument of today; and at much the same time the familiar 'upright' piano was developed.

In all these instruments the key is used as a lever to throw a hammer against the string(s) by means of a more or less complicated mechanism. Simultaneously it operates a felt damper, which leaves the strings when the key is depressed and returns to it when the key is released. The complete set of dampers can be raised, quite independently of the action of the keys, by means of a 'sustaining' pedal worked by the right foot, thus prolonging the sound of any notes played while the pedal remains down. On the pianoforte, and generally on the forte-piano, there is a second pedal, commonly known as the 'soft' pedal or *una corda*

(French: *sourdine*; German: *Verschiebung*), which is worked by the left foot and shifts the whole action slightly to one side, so that the hammers hit only two (or one) out of the three (or two) strings belonging to each note, or, on an upright piano, brings the hammers closer to the strings. (The lowest notes of the piano usually have only a single string each, and here the softening effect is produced by the string being struck by an unworn part of the hammer.) A third, central pedal (invented in 1862) is found on some modern instruments. If it is depressed when a note or chord is held down by the fingers, that same note or chord will alone be prolonged after the release of the key or keys, and quite independently of the use of the r.h. pedal.

The basic piano mechanism was devised by Bartolomeo Christofori (1665–1731). He produced his first instrument in Florence in about 1709, calling it a *gravicembalo col piano e forte* (harpsichord with loud and soft), and by 1726 had developed a more complex model complete with an *una corda* mechanism. Modifications of Christofori's action were adopted in other countries; and by 1745 J. S. Bach in Germany is known to have played on several of Gottfried Silbermann's instruments. (According to Bach's pupil Johann Friedrich Agricola he remained unenthusiastic about them, for he found their high register weak and their touch heavy.)

Heaviness of touch must have militated against the early popularity of the piano, for it was not until Silbermann's pupil Johann Andreas Stein developed the so-called Viennese action about 1773 that an instrument emerged with a light and reliable action, a well-matched treble and bass, and a pleasing though not particularly powerful singing tone. It had a compass of five octaves, from F_1 to f'''.

The Viennese action reached its peak of perfection around 1780 and continued in favour for more than a century after that. As early as 1759, however, English piano making had received a great impetus from the arrival in London of Johann Christian Bach, who, unlike his father Johann Sebastian, always preferred the piano to either the clavichord or the harpsichord. Makers such as Zumpe (another pupil of Silbermann), Broadwood, and Stodart gradually introduced their own improvements, and eventually outstripped their continental rivals. And finally the enthusiasm of Haydn, Clementi, and Dussek for English instruments was confirmed by Beethoven's warm welcome for the piano sent to him as a gift in 1818 by Thomas Broadwood.

From 1800 piano makers throughout Europe were mainly occupied in meeting the demand for a larger and more powerful instrument, which would be suitable for use in concert halls and capable of fulfilling the requirements of virtuosi such as Liszt and Thalberg. They gradually extended the compass of the keyboard (see Chapter 9, p. 168); and, as the tension (and hence the size) of the strings was increased, did their best to design frames that would be strong enough to support them. By mid-century their object was achieved through the introduction of the all-iron frame, high-tension strings, and heavy felt-covered hammers. In England Broadwood produced such an instrument for the Great Exhibition of 1851, and the firm of Steinway was making its own model in Hamburg four years later. As a result, the tonal character and touch of the instrument became completely altered, and the early fortepiano turned into what was virtually the pianoforte that we know today.

To sum up the tonal characteristics of the earlier stringed keyboard instruments:

1. The echiquier may have sounded not unlike a Hungarian cimbalom played without the dampers.

2. The clavichord is unique in its subtlety and delicacy. Like the piano, it can produce continuously graded dynamics: that is, a crescendo, a diminuendo, and different dynamics simultaneously in different voices. It is extremely sensitive to variations in touch, and can even, unlike any other keyboard instrument, produce a vibrato. Its power, however, is very limited.

3. The harpsichord, on the other hand, is comparatively powerful. It has a brilliant, incisive tone, whose strength and colour can be altered either by a change of manual or by means of stops (latterly pedals), and to a much lesser degree—as pointed out earlier—by differences of touch. The broader alterations can only be made in clearly defined steps; and any involving a change of stop requires an appreciable time to accomplish. Unlike the clavichord and piano, the harpsichord cannot produce a continuously graded range of dynamics, or a gradual crescendo or diminuendo. It is limited to one dynamic level at a time, except for the contrast that can be obtained by playing on a different manual with each hand.

4. The tone of the spinet is clear and brilliant, while that of the muselar type of virginals is rounded and more mellow. As neither instrument has any stops, the player has only a single tone colour at his disposal, apart from any slight changes he can effect by differences of touch.

5. None of the above instruments has a sustaining pedal.

6. The fortepiano has a tone that is clearer, lighter, and weaker than that of the modern piano. (Indeed at times it can be mistaken for a harpsichord.) It

can produce continuously graded dynamics, and has both a sustaining pedal and (generally) a *una corda* pedal.

Further Reading

(See the following in Suggestions for Further Reading, pp. 177 ff.)

Clutton, Cecil, 'Arnault's MS' (concerning the Echiquier).
Grove's Dictionary, under Clavichord, Harpsichord, Hydraulis, Organ, Pianoforte.
Harding, Rosamond E. M., *The Pianoforte*.
Russell, Raymond, *The Harpsichord and Clavichord*.
Sumner, William L., *The Organ*.

2 Musical Types and Forms

The musical types and forms used by the pre-Classical keyboard composers fall into two broad categories: those that are derived in some way from vocal music, and those that are purely instrumental in origin. The first group includes: (1) transcriptions or imitations of polyphonic vocal motets, or works derived therefrom; (2) pieces based on liturgical plainsong; (3) pieces based on chorales (i.e. metrical hymn tunes); and (4) arrangements or imitations of songs. To the second group belong: (5) preludes and toccatas; (6) dances, either single or in groups (i.e. suites); (7) illustrative or character pieces; (8) variations; and (9) sonatas.

Though the types are by no means exclusive, it will nevertheless be convenient to consider them separately, adding where necessary some hints concerning their performance.

I. TRANSCRIPTIONS OR IMITATIONS OF POLYPHONIC VOCAL MOTETS, and works derived therefrom, are of great importance, for they provide many of the commonest early instrumental forms.

Their ancestor was the *Canon*, in which two or more voices start successively but sing the same melodic line. If each entry begins on the same note it is termed a canon at the unison. (Thus a *Round* is a perpetual unison-canon in which each voice returns to the beginning as soon as it has completed the melody.) But the second voice may enter on other degrees of the scale, to produce a canon at the second, at the third, at the fourth, etc. Moreover, it may sing the melody *Inverted* (substituting upward intervals for downward, and vice versa), *Retrograde* (back to front, sometimes known as *Cancrizans*, i.e. 'crabwise'), in *Augmentation* (with doubled note values), in *Diminution* (with halved note values), or in some combination of these methods. Originally only one voice part was written out, together with a rubric, sometimes in the form of a puzzle (hence *Puzzle Canon*), to indicate where and how the remaining voice(s) should enter. This was, in fact, the 'canon' or rule that gave the form its name.

Fine examples for keyboard can be found in William Byrd's 'Pavan: Canon 2 in 1' (CE II, No. 74), where the top two parts are canonic, with the second starting a bar later and a fifth lower than the first; and in Bach's great 'Goldberg' Variations, where every third variation is a canon at a different interval, ranging from the unison to the ninth.

In the 16th-century vocal *Motet*, which evolved from the canon, successive portions of a text are set in imitative counterpoint. Each section may be built on a separate musical subject (known in England as a 'point of imitation', or simply a 'point': see Thomas Tallis's 'A Poynct', *MB*, No. 103; *EEKM* I, p. 25); or the different sections can be based either wholly or in part on rhythmic variants of the main subject; or a combination of the two methods can be used.

Some of the instrumental forms derived from the motet are: (a) the *Canzona francese*: an arrangement, strict or free, of a French *chanson*, usually light in character and sectional in structure, with either a fresh subject for each section, or a recurrence of the principal subject in some such sequence as A A B, A B A, A A B A, etc; (b) the *Canzona* or *Canzon*: an original piece similar to the foregoing; (c) the *Ricercare* (from the Italian word meaning 'to seek out', i.e. something recondite): similar to the canzona, but generally (though not invariably) more serious in character; (d) the *Fantasia*, *Fantasy*, or *Fancy*: yet another form similar to the canzona, and only very rarely a free, quasi-improvisatory piece such as the title often implied from the 18th century onwards; and (e) the later *Fugue*, described by Tovey as 'a texture the rules of which do not suffice to determine the shape of the composition as a whole' (but see p. 15).

Interpretation

When studying pieces of the above types it is helpful at first to define the structure by marking in pencil the beginning and end of each section.

Sections usually begin with the entry of a theme that differs significantly from the one preceding it; and they end with a well-defined cadence which may or may not overlap the following section. The different themes can be indicated by capital letters (A, B, C, etc.); the return of a theme by the repetition of its letter (e.g. A B A); and the end of a section by a sign such as ⌐. Variants of a theme can be distinguished by the addition of numerals (e.g. A, A1, A2, etc.); and a divided theme, whose components are developed separately, by the addition of superscript numerals (e.g. A^1, A^2).

When the overall structure has been mapped out thus, it is easier to see the relationship of one section to another, and to decide how the various themes should be articulated (see Chapter 4, Phrasing and Articulation). The following points may be borne in mind: (a) cadences that do not overlap the following section are more important than those that do; (b) they may at times need to be underlined with the help of a *rit.*; (c) movements containing no changes of time-signature are likely to be fairly constant in tempo, apart from small fluctuations that may be suggested by changes in texture or rhythmic movement; and (d) thematic contrasts can be heightened by contrasted articulation.

More varied markings will be required for a Fugue. The simplest type begins with an Exposition in which all the 'voices' or parts enter one by one, each with a statement of the theme. The entries generally alternate between tonic (these may be marked S, for Subject) and dominant (A, for Answer). (Though it need not concern the player, a 'real answer' is an exact transposition of the subject, whereas a 'tonal answer' adjusts some interval(s) of the subject in order to adapt it from the tonic to the dominant part of the scale, or vice versa.) Further marks may or may not be required for the exposition. If the 1st voice accompanies the 2nd voice's entry with a counterpoint that reappears later with the theme, it should be labelled CS (for Counter-Subject); while E (for Episode) can indicate any passage that separates entries of the theme, whether based on new material or old.

The subsequent growth of a fugue is unpredictable; but it can be clarified for study with the help of the marks already suggested, plus E2, E3, E4, etc., for fresh episodes; St, for Strettos, i.e. overlapping entries of the subject; and Inv, Aug, and Dim, for Inversion, Augmentation, and Diminution, as described earlier (p. 13).

In a double fugue—i.e. where a second theme appears when the music is well under way, and is combined with the first theme, either immediately (as in Bach's '48' Bk. II, No. 23 in B) or eventually (as in the '48' Bk. II, No. 18 in G sharp minor)—the two subjects may be distinguished as S1 and S2. In a triple fugue, such as '48' Bk. II, No. 14 in F sharp minor, S3 can be added; and in a quadruple fugue, S4. Twin subjects, which are announced by two voices before the entry of the answer, may be marked S^1 and S^2. They are rare in keyboard music (Bach has none), but are found for example in Handel's Fuga I in G minor, CE III, No. 1.

2. In most PLAINSONG SETTINGS one contrapuntal strand of the composition is supplied by a liturgical plainsong melody, while the remaining voices weave contrapuntal figuration or imitation around it. The borrowed part is called the *cantus firmus* (literally, 'fixed song') and is generally, though not invariably, confined to a single voice. It may appear in long, equal notes:

Ex. 4 John Taverner, 'In Nomine' (*MB*, No. 35; *EEKM* I, p. 22)
cantus firmus in the alto.

or in ornamented form (i.e. 'coloured'):

Ex. 5 William Blitheman, 'Christe qui lux' (*MB*, No. 22; *EEKM* I, p. 28):
cantus firmus in the alto (original plainsong shown above).

Or it may be treated as little more than a point of departure, as in John Redford's 'Eterne Rex Altissime' (*MB*, No. 26; *EEKM* I, p. 24), where the complete plainsong, partly decorated and partly undecorated, occupies no more than eight bars of the tenor part out of a total of twenty-one.

The Taverner 'In Nomine' shown in Ex. 4, above, is of particular interest, for it was the source of the countless instrumental 'In Nomines' that were written in England during the succeeding century and a half. The version shown is a contemporary keyboard arrangement of the 'In Nomine Domini' section of the Benedictus from Taverner's Mass based on the plainsong antiphon 'Gloria Tibi Trinitas':

Ex. 6 Plainsong antiphon, 'Gloria Tibi Trinitas'

The vocal original (see *Tudor Church Music* I, p. 148) became so popular that subsequent pieces founded on the same plainsong were more often known by the title 'In Nomine' than by the more accurate 'Gloria Tibi Trinitas'.

Interpretation

Since the main musical (as distinct from liturgical) function of a plainsong *cantus firmus* was to provide the composer with a basic structure or thread around which his ideas might crystallize, its melodic aspect was rarely important. In performance, therefore, it should merge with the other textural elements of the music.

Certain plainsong settings omit every alternate verse or group of verses of the text. This type was intended for *alternatim* performance during the liturgy, when the missing verses were sung to unison plainsong by the unaccompanied choir. The precise way in which the plainsong was shared between choir and organ varied from work to work; but in an *alternatim* Mass, for example, the Gloria would always begin in the usual way, with the priest intoning the words 'Gloria in excelsis Deo'; the organ might then enter with an ornamented setting of the plainsong for the words 'et in terra pax hominibus bonae voluntatis'; this could be followed by the choir singing the undecorated plainsong for 'laudamus te'; and so on, with organ and choir alternating for the remainder of the Gloria.

3. In Protestant Germany, Lutheran CHORALES or hymn tunes, such as that shown in Ex. 7, were used more often than plainsong to provide *cantus firmi.*

Ex. 7 Chorale, 'Ach Herr, mich armen Sünder'

[Words: Cyriakus Scheegass, 1597; trans. C. Sanford Terry]

They generally appear in liturgical contexts, such as Cantatas or the Chorale Preludes that provided interludes during the church service; but they also turn up occasionally in more homely surroundings. The melody shown in Ex. 7, familiar from Bach's harmonizations in the *St Matthew Passion*, is used in Johann Kuhnau's Suonata Quarta for chamber organ or harpsichord (*EGKM* I, p. 38) to represent King Hezekiah's prayers and confidence in God. And, more surprisingly, Diderik Buxtehude's Variations on 'Auf meinen lieben Gott' (*EGKM* I, p. 59) are each based on a different type of dance.

Interpretation

Chorales, either plain or decorated, are more often used melodically than is plainsong. Thus in performance they often require to stand out somewhat from the surrounding texture. Their precise degree of importance must be judged in each instance according to the musical function they fulfil.

In the vocal originals breathing-points were generally indicated by pause marks (⌒) as shown in Ex. 7, above. These are often reproduced in instrumental settings; but since their main function was to act as structural signposts, they were rarely meant to be taken literally.

4. ARRANGEMENTS OR IMITATIONS OF SONGS comprise straightforward keyboard versions of a vocal original, with or without added variations of one kind or another (see section 8, below); and also purely instrumental pieces built on similar lines.

The latter include ritornello-type movements, which were direct descendants of the operatic aria as developed by Alessandro Scarlatti and his school. Such an aria is based on the contrast between a powerful but impersonal group (the orchestral tutti) and a weaker but more expressive individual (the soloist). In essence, it opens with an orchestral paragraph, or ritornello, stating the principal thematic material in the tonic key. The soloist then enters, either with a short restatement of some of the same material or with an entirely fresh idea. The orchestra responds with part of the ritornello, which encourages the soloist to embark on a longer flight. This is likely to lead away from the tonic to some nearly-related key, which is duly confirmed by the transposed orchestral ritornello, or part of it. Thereafter, soloist and orchestra continue in alternation and combination, with reappearances of the ritornello (in various keys) to act as pillars that support the whole structure. Finally the tonic is reached once more, and a full recapitulation of the ritornello rounds off the movement.

When a structure of this type is translated into purely instrumental terms the result is the early 18th-century concerto-type movement. The place of the vocalist is taken by an instrumental soloist, or by a small group of soloists (the *concertino*), while the orchestral tutti (the *ripieno*) fulfils the same function as before. Moreover, soloist and orchestra can be represented by two contrasted manuals on either organ or harpsichord; or even by a single-manual instrument if the basic contrasts are sufficiently apparent.

Interpretation

J. S. Bach himself marked most of the necessary changes of manual in the only two solo harpsichord works of this type that he published during his lifetime: the Italian Concerto, BWV 971, and the French Overture or Partita in B minor, BWV 831. In them the words *forte* and *piano* indicate respectively the lower manual ('orchestra') and the upper ('soloist'). The markings are not altogether complete in either work, but it is not difficult to supply the few that are missing, particularly when it is remembered that a movement is always understood to begin *forte* unless otherwise marked.

These two works should be used as models when interpreting unmarked movements of the same type, such as the Preludes of Bach's English Suites Nos. 2–6. It is important to remember that changes of manual do not always occur simultaneously in both hands; and that they must only be made at musically logical points (i.e. never in the middle of a phrase).

5. Of purely instrumental forms, the PRELUDE and TOCCATA are closely related. The prelude was originally a short improvisation played on the organ to indicate to the intoning priest or the choir the pitch and 'tone' or mode (see Chapter 7, below) of the music they were about to sing. Similar pieces were later written down for the benefit for those who were learning to improvise them, or were unable to do so; and it is these short works that provide the first known examples of keyboard music that is neither a dance nor dependent on some vocal model. (See Ileborgh's *Tablatur*, 1448, and Paumann's *Fundamentum*, 1452, in *CEKM* I, pp. 28 and 50–51, and the *Buxheimer Orgelbuch* of c. 1460–70.) Such preludes might include a brilliant flourish or two, and this led by extension to the longer toccata (from the Italian *toccare*, to touch), which in the first place was a keyboard work in several contrasted sections designed to display the varied capabilities of a player and his instrument.

Their improvisatory origin is often reflected in both types of work—

particularly in French 'unmeasured' preludes (see pp. 23–8). But the title 'Prelude' was also used for any other kind of introductory piece, e.g. Bach's Forty-Eight Preludes and Fugues; and a toccata eventually became synonymous with a *moto perpetuo* (see the toccatas of Czerny, Schumann, Debussy, Ravel, etc.).

Interpretation
When either a prelude or a toccata shows traces of its improvisatory origin, this should be reflected in performance. The precise degree of freedom needed depends on the musical content. Passages and sections that lack a clearly defined theme, or consist mainly of brilliant flourishes, should be wayward in rhythm; whereas those that are built on definite themes will tend to establish a tempo and keep to it for as long as the theme persists. In the freer sections the effect should be that of the player tentatively feeling his way towards some more positive thematic idea, or of displaying his manual dexterity; and in the stricter sections, that he is exploring the beauties and possibilities of the particular idea or ideas that he has discovered. Sections will often dissolve and merge, rather than being clearly separated like the movements of a suite; yet the performer must always bear in mind their different functions, so that he may show both their interrelationship and the essential contrast between them.

The prefaces to Girolamo Frescobaldi's *Toccate e partite*, 1614, and *Il primo libro di capricci*, 1624, contain instructions to performers which may be summarized (with some additional comments within square brackets) as follows:

i. The tempo of a toccata does not remain unchanged throughout, but varies (like that of a madrigal) according to the mood of the music: now slow, now fast, with pauses where necessary. [Most likely this refers mainly to tempo changes between one section and another, though local fluctuations would not be excluded.]

ii. If a work is too long, self-contained sections may be played separately, provided they end in a suitable key [*i.e.* the one in which they began].

iii. Harpsichord toccatas should begin very slowly, with the chords played *arpeggiando* to make up for the instrument's lack of sustaining power. Suspensions and discords in the middle of a piece should also at times be played *arpeggiando*. [The *arpeggiando* intended is not the quick, brilliant kind suited to Bach's Chromatic Fantasia, etc., but the slow, meditative repetition of individual notes of a chord such as is needed to sustain the long-held notes in

the Sarabande of the English Suite No. 3 in G minor. For example, the
opening of Frescobaldi's Toccata No. 7:

Ex. 8

might be played

[Adagio]

   iv. Pause on the last note both of shakes and of passage-work, even if small
in value, as this will avoid confusing one passage with another.

   v. The ends of musical sections should be played *ritardando*, even when the
note-values are small. Such endings are [sometimes] shown by minim chords in
both hands. [This is to clarify the structure of toccatas, canzonas, ricercars, etc.
It obviously would not apply to a dance-movement, whose very nature demands
an unchanging pulse in all but the final bars.]

   vi. A shake in one hand should not coincide note for note with passage-
work in the other, [even when written out in identical note-values]. The shake
should be played quickly and the passage-work more expressively. [This shows
that the number of repercussions in a written-out shake is schematic and may
be increased at will.]

   vii. If a passage has quavers in one hand and semiquavers in the other it
should not be played too fast, and the rhythm of the semiquavers should be
altered to approximately ♫♫ . [See Chapter 6, Rhythmic Conventions,
p. 100.]

   viii. If a passage has semiquavers [or demi-semiquavers] in both hands you
should dwell on the preceding note, then play the passage boldly in order to
show your dexterity.

ix. Sections of partitas and toccatas which include notes of small value or expressive ornamentation should be played slowly, plainer sections more quickly, the choice of tempo being left to the good taste of the performer. [Care is needed here, for small note-values can also imply a quicker sense of movement, even if the beat is slower.]

A century later François Couperin wrote of his own preludes in the treatise *L'Art de toucher le clavecin*, 1716:

> Whoever uses these non-improvised preludes should play them freely, without attaching too much importance to the exact time—unless I have indicated the contrary by the word *Mesuré*.

In addition to these and to genuinely improvised preludes there were imitations of the latter—the puzzling-looking 'unmeasured' preludes written by various French composers from Louis Couperin (François's uncle) to Dandrieu. (See Ex. 9a, below.)

Unmeasured preludes consist essentially of long strings of unbarred semi-breves, whose rhythmic interpretation is left to the taste of the performer; but smaller note-values are sometimes introduced, and occasionally a section in some normally barred rhythm may occur. Though no contemporary instructions have survived concerning their performance, it is clear that they stem from similar lute pieces, and that these imitate the extemporization of a lutenist as he checks the tuning of his instrument, gets the 'feel' of his surroundings, and establishes the key, and sometimes the mood, of the work he is about to perform. Their rhythmic interpretation is therefore expected to vary from occasion to occasion, and should never be exactly the same twice running.

When studying such pieces it will be helpful to bear in mind the following points:

i. Semibreves in unmeasured preludes stand for all note-values. When smaller notes than semibreves occur, their values are not meant to be read strictly, either with reference to one another or to the semibreves.

ii. An accidental generally, though not invariably, applies only to the note it precedes.

iii. The printed order of the notes should usually be followed, those in vertical alignment being played together. (Sometimes the latter are joined by a plain or dotted line.) Ornaments provide an exception to the second part of this rule, for as usual they coincide with the pulse and therefore displace the main note from its expected position.

Ex. 9 Louis Couperin, Prélude in A minor (Paris, Bib. Nat. Vm⁷ 675, f.12ᵛ)

iv. Slurs are used for three different purposes: (a) to phrase together a group of notes (e.g. Ex. 9a, b.7, l.h.); (b) to indicate an appoggiatura—most two-note slurs belong to this type (*idem*, b.3, r.h. C to B, and l.h. A to G sharp); and (c) to show that a note, or several notes, should be sustained for approximately the length of the slur (*idem*, b.1 for a six-part chord; and b.5, r.h., for a single note, E, carried over three 'bars'). N.B.: A slur joining two identical notes must not be mistaken for a tie. As can be seen from section (c) above, the second note would not be needed to obtain a tied effect; it should therefore always be restruck.

Since slurs of every type are sometimes inaccurately placed in both manuscript and print, a certain latitude must be allowed to their interpretation.

v. The student's first concern should be to establish the prelude's harmonic structure. In order to do this he must distinguish between the several different functions of the l.h. notes: i.e. decide whether they are (a) the bass of the harmony (see Ex. 9a, b.1, note 1; b.2, note 1; and b.3, note 2); (b) bass appoggiaturas—these are generally the first of a pair of slurred notes (*idem*, b.3, note 1); (c) melodic or decorative bass notes (*idem*, b.7); (d) an inner part of an arpeggiated chord (*idem*, b.1, notes 2 and 3); or (e) an inner voice such as the tenor (*idem*, b.10, last 4 notes).

When making such an analysis of the l.h. part it is helpful to add a small pencil tick immediately in front of each note belonging to class (a), and in front of each appoggiatura-pair belonging to class (b). It is then a fairly simple matter, by following the pencil ticks and reducing the remaining l.h. and r.h. notes to their basic chords, to play through the progressions that form the harmonic skeleton of the whole piece. (See Ex. 9b.)

After the basic harmonies have been played through several times, the function and relative importance of the various progressions and cadences will readily become apparent. E.g. in Ex. 9 the first harmonic landmark is the shift to the dominant, E minor, in b.6. (The $\frac{6}{3}$ chord on G sharp in b.3 is only a local inflection.) The harmony then slips down to the relative major (b.9), and from there climbs stepwise to the middle of b.11, where a lengthy harping on and around the dominant prepares us for the final tonic in b.16.

The structure that emerges in this particular piece is not unlike a miniature version of the normal bipartite dance-form, in which there is a general movement from the tonic to a more-or-less central cadence on the dominant or some other closely related key (marked by the double-bar), followed by a gradual return to the tonic (see section vi, below). This can be seen even more clearly in some larger-scale preludes, where the 'central' cadence is much stronger than in this example.

vi. Once the harmonic structure has been established, the next step is to analyse the melodic and decorative elements. In order to do this the player must distinguish between the several different functions of the r.h. notes: i.e. decide whether they are: (a) parts of the melodic or decorative soprano line (see Ex. 9a, b.8); (b) appoggiaturas—again often the first of a pair of slurred notes (*idem*, b.3, C); (c) an inner voice such as the alto (*idem*, b.14, last 3 notes, and b.15, last 2 notes); (d) parts of an arpeggiated chord (*idem*, b.1); or (e) parts of a decorated arpeggio (*idem*, b.4, last 4 notes, the G sharp being the decoration).

Naturally these categories overlap at times: e.g. in the example given of a decorated arpeggio (e), the 2nd note, G sharp, is an appoggiatura (b). But the fluency of the player's interpretation will depend on the speed with which he can recognize them all.

vii. The final step is to supply the missing rhythms and phrases of the prelude—always remembering that their details vary from performance to performance. In this connection the following points should be borne in mind: (a) a prelude is generally best interpreted within the framework of a fairly constant beat, without which it is apt to sound incoherent; (b) its bar-lengths may vary, in keeping with its free, improvisatory character; (c) its note-values should be nicely balanced between variety and regularity; (d) the harmonic structure must always be clearly preserved, the relative importance of each cadence and progression being reflected in its rhythmic treatment; (e) the bass notes already marked with a pencil tick (see section v (a) and (b), above) are likely to occur on 'beats', and so are melodically important notes and ornaments, as these generally imply accents; (f) the changing contrapuntal tensions between the soprano part and the bass, and the different functions of the remaining r.h. and l.h. notes (see sections v and vi above), must also be reflected in the rhythmic treatment; (g) sequential passages tend to fall into regular rhythmic patterns; (h) a group of conjunct notes often indicates a flourish in short note-values (see Ex. 9, b.4, r.h., and b.13, l.h.); and (i) the second note of an identical pair is more likely to be accented than the first (*idem*, r.h., b.5 As, and b.6 F sharps).

viii. The preludes must not be rushed. They require the amplitude and meditative quality that is natural to an improvisation. (In the present realization the slow metronome mark must be borne in mind when reading the semi-quavers and demi-semiquavers.) In performance the effect should be poetical, yet imbued with a typically French sense of neatness and clarity. When in doubt about any particular point, the player must rely on his knowledge of other contemporary French harpsichord (and if possible lute) music; and, as always, on his own instinct and musical feeling. Finally, it cannot be stressed sufficiently strongly that the realization suggested in Ex. 9c should *not* be followed slavishly. It is only one of countless possibilities, since there are as many different interpretations of this type of movement as there are performances.

6. DANCES long remained one of the most popular of all instrumental types. Originally intended as no more than an accompaniment to dancing, they later came to be written and enjoyed for their own sake.

The earliest surviving keyboard dance, and one of the most important instrumental forms of the 13th and 14th centuries, is the *Estampie*. It consists of several sections known as *puncti* (A, B, C, etc.), each of which is repeated. *Punctus* A has a 1st-time ending (*ouvert* = y), and a 2nd-time ending (*clos* = z). Each subsequent *punctus* recapitulates part of A, the first time round with its y-ending and the second time round with its z-ending, thus producing the pattern:

Ay, Az; B+part of Ay, B+part of Az;
C+part of Ay, C+part of Az; etc.

The only known keyboard estampies are found in the earliest of all keyboard sources, the *Robertsbridge Fragment* of *c.* 1320 (see *CEKM* I, Nos. 1–3).

Next in order of date comes the French *Basse Danse* of the 15th century, which may have originated at the court of Burgundy. In many sources two such dances are paired together, the first in a moderate duple time and the second in a quicker triple. This double contrast of rhythm and mood proved so satisfying that it reappears in many other paired dances, such as the *Branle Simple* & *Branle Gay* of France, the *Passamezzo* & *Saltarello* of Italy, the *Tanz* & *Nachtanz* of Germany, and the ubiquitous *Pavan* & *Galliard* with their quicker companions the *Alman* & *Coranto*. Most of the dances are bipartite; but Pavans and Galliards are generally, though not invariably, tripartite.

These terms, bipartite and tripartite, are used in the present book in order to avoid the words 'binary' and 'ternary', which have been applied to musical forms in conflicting ways in the past. The structures they describe are enormously important,-for they recur continually throughout the history of music.

A *Bipartite* structure is one that falls into two clearly defined sections, either or both of which may or may not be repeated. There are two distinct types. In one the central cadence is *not* on the tonic—this is the *open* type since it implies some continuation (cf. the *ouvert* ending of a *punctus* in an Estampie);

in the other the central cadence *is* on the tonic—the *closed* type which arouses no immediate expectation of a continuation (cf. the *clos* ending of a *punctus*).

The *open* type is the commoner of the two, and appears not only in simple melodic form but also in larger movements containing several distinct thematic elements, such as the majority of Scarlatti's 555 Sonatas and almost half of the Preludes in Book II of Bach's 48 Preludes and Fugues. Eventually it evolves into Classical Sonata-form (see section 9, pp. 35–7).

The *closed* type leads to *Tripartite* structures falling into three clearly defined sections. They can be either simple, as in an A B A movement (but *not* an ‖: A :‖: BA :‖ one, which is clearly bipartite); or else compound, as in Bourrée I–Bourrée II–[Bourrée I], and the later Scherzo–Trio–[Scherzo], where each component is generally in itself a bipartite structure of either the open or closed type. Through extension they produce Rondos of one kind or another: e.g. the simple A B A C . . . A form, or the more complex types discussed later (see under Classical, p. 38).

In dances of the 16th and 17th centuries certain harmonic patterns appeared so frequently that they became recognized throughout Europe. The most familiar was the *Passamezzo antico*, referred to by Shakespeare in *Twelfth Night*, 5.i.205, as the 'passy measures'. In essence it consists of a common-chord progression on the following bass, or some variation of it:

Ex. 10 The *Passamezzo antico*

Other established formulae were the *Passamezzo moderno*, known in England as the *Quadran*:

Ex. 11 The *Passamezzo moderno* or *Quadran*

the *Romanesca*, and the *Folia*:

Ex. 12 The *Romanesca*

Ex. 13 The *Folia*

(Curiously enough, Frescobaldi's 'Partita sopra Folia', CE I, No. 18, is based on an altogether different harmonic pattern.)

During the 17th century the court ballet of France added a large number of regional and other dances to the already established *Allemande* (= Alman) and *Courante* (= Coranto). Some of these were the *Minuet* (in moderate $\frac{3}{4}$ time), the *Sarabande* (a slow $\frac{4}{4}$), the *Gavotte* (fairly quick $\frac{4}{4}$, with a half-bar upbeat), the *Bourrée* (quicker $\frac{2}{2}$, with a crotchet upbeat), the *Passepied* (a quick $\frac{3}{8}$ or $\frac{6}{8}$), and the *Loure* (a slowish, dotted $\frac{6}{4}$); to which were added aliens such as the *Polonaise* (a moderate $\frac{3}{4}$) and the *Anglaise* ($\frac{2}{2}$); together with movements originally unconnected with the dance, e.g. the *Air*, borrowed from opera; the *Rondeau*, a descendant of the monophonic rondeau of the Trouvères, but shaped more simply A B A C A D . . . A; and the *French Overture*, an innovation of Lully's consisting of a slow, majestic introduction in dotted rhythm, followed by a bustling movement in fugal style.

The organization of a more or less standard *Suite* form appears to have been initiated by Johann Jakob Froberger (1616–1667). The basic plan consists of four contrasted national dances: the *Allemande* from Germany (now a slow $\frac{4}{4}$); the *Corrente* from Italy (a flowing $\frac{3}{4}$) or the *Courante* from France (a more complex $\frac{3}{2}$, whose six crotchets in a bar could be grouped as either three twos or—particularly at cadences—two threes—a type of cross-rhythm known as *hemiola*); the *Sarabande* from Spain (a stately $\frac{3}{4}$); and the *Gigue*, or jig, from England (a brisk $\frac{3}{8}$, $\frac{6}{8}$, or $\frac{12}{8}$—but see also the C-time gigues discussed in Chapter 6: Rhythmic Conventions, under Binary Notation for Ternary). Froberger originally placed the gigue before the sarabande, or else omitted it altogether; but when his Suites were published posthumously in 1693 the order was changed ('mis en meilleur ordre'), with the gigue coming at the end. To this basic four-movement plan later composers added further dances, known collectively in France as *Galanteries* and in Germany as *Galanterien* (literally, 'courtesies'), which could either follow or precede the gigue. Bach generally chose the latter alternative, and at one time or another used all the dances listed in the preceding paragraph. Each of his English Suites, with the exception of the first, begins with a large-scale prelude in ritornello-form (see section 4, pp. 19–20); while his Partitas—a title used not only for suites but also for sets of variations—each have an introductory movement in some special style, ranging from a two-part fantasia to a full-blown toccata.

Interpretation

Since the aim of most suites is to provide a group of movements to be performed as a sequence, it may generally be assumed that every dance will differ from its neighbour(s) in both tempo and mood—always excepting pairs of identical dances (see below), where the mood changes but not the tempo; and *Doubles* (see below), where both tempo and mood are likely to remain constant. Some very long suites, however, appear to be no more than collections of pieces in a single key, from which the player can choose a group of whatever length he requires. For example, the twenty-three movements of Couperin's Ordre 2 could hardly have been intended for complete performance.

Dance movements do *not* require a *rit.* before every double-bar. To think otherwise is to misunderstand Frescobaldi's dictum that the ends of musical sections should be played *ritardando*. Here he was writing specifically of toccatas and capriccios: not of dances, whose very nature demands an unchanging pulse in all but the final bars.

The notation of repeats in early sources (and not only of dance movements) was often haphazard. What looks like a repeat-sign may be no more than an ornamental double-bar (as in the *FWVB*), and what looks like a plain double-bar may in fact be an indication for a repeat. Furthermore, 1st- and 2nd-time bars, if differentiated at all, are apt to show little regard for either logic or arithmetic.

Since modern editions do not always adjust these types of notation to conform with present-day practice, it is as well to bear in mind the following points: (a) it was usual to repeat each section of a dance movement, unless written-out divisions (i.e. varied repeats) were already included in the text; (b) if there were no written-out divisions the player was at liberty, when the music was not complex, to extemporize his own decorated repeats; (c) short dances could be repeated *in toto*; and (d) minor adjustments to the text were often needed in order to make a single bar act as both 1st- and 2nd-time bars.

In French music the word *Reprise* indicates the beginning of the second half of the piece. In addition, a *Petite Reprise* is sometimes marked towards the end of the second half. This is an extra repeat of the concluding bars (generally either four or eight), which may be either written out in full or (more often) indicated by a sign.

In some suites two or more dances of the same type appear side by side—particularly courantes and the various *galanteries*; furthermore, a dance is sometimes followed by its *double* or variation.

Pairs of *galanteries* together form tripartite structures (A B A), like the more familiar minuet and trio. Thus Bourrées I and II in Bach's English Suite No. 1 in A are played consecutively with all the marked repeats, and are then followed by a return to Bourrée I *without* its repeats.

Courantes, on the other hand, appear to have been played separately, to judge by the use in certain sources of *custos* or 'directs'—the ↶ signs added at the end of lines, or before repeats, to indicate the notes that follow. It is not clear, however, whether all the Courantes of a group were meant to be played—Chambonnières has as many as three in a row—or whether the performer was expected to make a choice.

The evidence concerning *doubles* is conflicting. In many cases the *custos* show that the dance and its *double* were played consecutively, and with all repeats. But a different and more practical sequence is indicated in at least one source, Paris Conserv. MS Rés. 18–223, f. 51ᵛ–52ʳ, where Chambonnières's sarabande 'O beau jardin' is followed by a *double* added probably by d'Anglebert. Here the *custos* and repeat signs show that the equivalent strain of the *double* should be substituted for each repeat of the sarabande, thus:

Sarabande, str. 1—Double, str. 1—Sarabande, str. 2—Double, str. 2.

This sequence, which works well in performance, was probably also intended in the Sarabande and 'Les agréments de la même Sarabande' in Bach's English Suites Nos. 2 and 3.

In the English Suite No. 1 in A it is less certain how Courante I and Courante II with its two Doubles should be treated. If the group is played complete, and with all repeats, it sounds far too long in relation to the rest of the suite. Failing certain knowledge of what was intended, the following scheme is offered as a workable solution to the problem:

> Courante I, str. 1—Courante I, str. 2—
> Courante II, str. 1—Double I, str. 1—Courante II, str. 2—Double I, str. 2—
> Double II, str. 1—Double II, str. 2.

This interpretation is based in part on the sequence of repeats found in the Gigue of the English Suite No. 2 in A minor (AA BB AB), and probably also intended in certain allemandes by Chambonnières.

In French pieces that consist of a *Première* and *Seconde Partie*—and occasionally a *Troisième* and even a *Quatrième*—a *da capo* is marked in some but not in others; yet the latter often sound incomplete without some sort of recapitulation. When nothing is marked, the player must decide for himself what is required. If a *da capo* is made, however, it should include the whole of the *Première Partie* when the latter is bipartite. With a lengthy rondeau, on the other hand, it is generally sufficient to recapitulate no more than the opening refrain—as Couperin himself indicates in his 'L'Épineuse' (*Pièces de clavecin* IV, Ordre 26).

It will be convenient at this point to mention some notational peculiarities of the *Fitzwilliam Virginal Book*, though they are not confined to dance movements. The copyist of the manuscript, Francis Tregian, generally numbered the sections of a piece, and often marked varied repeats with the sign *Rep.* (This helpful practice has been copied by some modern editors.) He also had the curious habit of ending a piece with a calligraphically ornamental breve chord, whether required by the music or not. (Variant texts always omit the chord when it is not needed musically.) Since this idiosyncrasy is reproduced in the modern complete edition, it is important to remember that not every final bar in the *FWVB* was meant to be played. The rule is roughly as follows: if the final breve chord of a piece resolves the melody or harmony, or completes the expected rhythmic scheme, it should be played; otherwise it should be omitted.

7. ILLUSTRATIVE or CHARACTER PIECES were specially popular in France and England, but were also written elsewhere. Their aim was to provide a musical equivalent of the mood, object, person, or event indicated by the title, and they ranged from the Battle pieces of William Byrd and Girolamo Frescobaldi, through 'portraits' such as Couperin's 'Les Tricoteuses' (The Knitters), to Bach's 'Capriccio on the Departure of a Beloved Brother'. French

composers often gave illustrative titles to dance movements, either instead of, or in addition to, the name of the dance itself.

8. VARIATIONS of different kinds—melodic, harmonic, and sometimes rhythmic—are of great importance, for they provide one of the most obvious ways of extending a musical idea.

In the dances and song arrangements of the English virginalists, for example, the principle was applied in either or both of two ways. Firstly, the repeat of each strain of a tune could be varied instead of being left unaltered; and secondly, the complete tune, with either varied or unvaried repeats, could serve as a theme for a set of variations.

Another type of variation is related to the plainsong setting (see section 2, above). Here, however, the *cantus firmus* is supplied by repetitions of the ascending and descending notes of part of the diatonic scale—often a section known as a Hexachord, which comprises six consecutive diatonic notes with a single semitone interval in the middle: e.g. GAB CDE. Like the plainsong *cantus firmus*, the series is generally set out in long equal notes; and though it usually remains constant in overall pitch, it too may modulate, as in John Bull's remarkable 'Ut, re, mi, fa, sol, la' (*FWVB* I, No. 51), in which the hexachord begins successively on each of the twelve degrees of the chromatic scale.

In the *Ground-bass* or *Ground*—a type of variation of which Purcell was specially fond—a short, continuously repeated bass line provides the foundation for an ever-changing superstructure. Allied forms are the *Chaconne* and *Passacaglia*, in which the recurring element is either the bass or a series of harmonies, as in Bach's Passacaglia in C minor for organ. (In France the titles Chaconne and Passacaille were also applied to large-scale rondeaux: e.g. the Passacaille from Couperin's Ordre 8 in B minor.)

Interpretation
In sets of variations that contain changes of time-signature—such as Bach's vast 'Goldberg' Variations—there will very likely be an equal number of tempo changes, and probably more. On the other hand, works that have no change of time-signature are less likely to require changes of tempo. In some of the latter, however, there is such a wide range of note-values, or of mood, that it is impossible to find one tempo that fits every variation equally satisfactorily: and here there can be no doubt that various tempi were intended by the composer.

Whichever type of work is concerned, the player's aim should be to convey not only its inherent contrasts, but also its cumulative effect and overall span; and at all costs to prevent it from disintegrating into a series of unrelated fragments. The work itself will show whether this can best be achieved by preserving a uniform tempo throughout, or, on the contrary, by judiciously employing whatever changes are implied by the music.

9. The word SONATA originally signified no more than a 'sound piece' as opposed to a cantata or 'sung piece'. In the 16th and 17th centuries it was given both to single movements (often in bipartite form) and to groups of two or more movements embodying the familiar contrasts of tempo and mood. Two notable types (though confined to concerted music) were the *Sonata da chiesa* (church sonata) and the *Sonata da camera* (chamber sonata). The first consisted typically of a slow opening movement, a fugal allegro, a cantabile slow movement, and a lively finale; the second resembled the suite in being mainly devoted to dance movements. Johann Kuhnau's *Frische Früchte oder sieben Suonaten*, 1696, was the earliest publication in which the title was used for a keyboard solo as distinct from an ensemble work. The classical 'Viennese' sonata, which did not emerge until the mid-18th century, is discussed below.

CLASSICAL

The most important forms used by Classical composers are all associated with the sonata—and also, of course, with symphonies, trios, quartets, etc., which are 'sonatas' involving more than two players. In the Classical sense such a work consists of at least two, generally three, and sometimes four contrasted movements, of which the first and last share the same tonic. The usual sequence in a four-movement sonata is shown in the following table, together with the forms most often employed:

i.	Quick:	Sonata-form (sometimes known as '1st-movement form').
ii.	Slow:	Sonata-form (with or without a development section); Bipartite form (A BA); Tripartite form (A B A); Rondo; Variations.
iii.	Quick-ish	Minuet & trio, or Scherzo & trio (bipartite units within a tripartite whole).
iv.	Quick:	Rondo; Sonata-form; Variations.

(Note that the term 'sonata-form' refers only to a type of movement, not to the work as a whole. In some sonatas the minuet & trio, or scherzo & trio, precede the slow movement.)

A typical SONATA-FORM movement consists of the following elements:

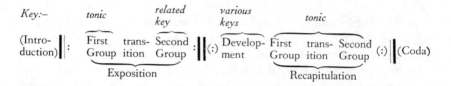

An introduction is not an essential part of the scheme and is rare in solo sonatas, but a coda is much more common. Concerning the repeat-signs, see below under *Interpretation*.

The misleading terms 'first and second subjects' have here been avoided, for there can be any number of clearly defined themes in either group. Moreover, the two groups can share the same thematic material—this is not unusual in Haydn—since the contrast between them is basically tonal rather than thematic. The section labelled Development may in fact develop themes, or parts of themes, from the Exposition; but it may equally well introduce material that is entirely new. Once again the thematic aspect is secondary, since the structural function of this section is to provide the kind of tonal contrasts that intensify the listener's anticipation of a return of the First Group in the tonic key. Some slow movements omit the development altogether in order to avoid excessive length.

Interpretation

A major problem in performing sonata-form movements, particularly those containing dramatically disparate elements, is to preserve the sense of overall span while at the same time indicating the constituent parts. The contrasts between themes must be given due weight, yet never at the expense of the structure as a whole. Furthermore, each section must be presented as the logical outcome of those that have gone before. A basic tempo—or at least the *impression* of a basic tempo—is generally required (see Chapter 3, Tempo: pp. 46–7), though there will almost certainly be subtle variations within that framework.

If a theme reappears it is important to note whether it has been changed in any way: e.g. has been decorated, or (even more significant) given a new harmonic twist. Such alterations always indicate a change of meaning which must be made clear in performance. A specially sensitive area in this respect is the middle of the Recapitulation, where the transition between First Group and Second is often expanded, or intensified harmonically, in order to bring the return of the Second Group into the tonic. (A simplified type of sonata-form avoids this significant moment by recapitulating the First Group in whatever key automatically brings the Second Group into the tonic, as in the first movement of Schubert's 'Trout' Quintet, D. 667.)

With regard to repeats: it was at first usual for both sections of a sonata-form movement to be repeated; but as works grew longer the second repeat was often ignored by players as being more a convention than a necessity; and finally composers left it out altogether.

In present-day performance the repeat of the exposition is the more likely to be required, not only from the structural point of view, but also because it gives the listener a second chance to absorb the thematic material. Moreover, it sometimes includes 1st-time bars of great significance; e.g. in the 1st movement of Schubert's Sonata in B flat, D.960, whose length might otherwise suggest the omission of the repeat. The 'second half' repeat is less likely to be needed; but in certain cases it is essential, even in works as late as Beethoven's Sonata in F sharp, Op. 78, for without it the movement will sound lop-sided and inconclusive. Each case must be judged on its own merits.

BIPARTITE and TRIPARTITE FORMS. As pointed out earlier (see section 6, pp. 28–9), and as shown by the table on the preceding page, sonata-form is in fact a greatly expanded Bipartite form of the open type. Shorter and simpler examples, either open or closed, can be found in almost any minuet, scherzo, or trio. When a minuet & trio, or scherzo & trio, are viewed as a whole, however, they constitute a Tripartite form (e.g. minuet—trio—[minuet]); as does the A B A type of slow movement found in Beethoven's Sonata in E flat, Op. 7, and in Schubert's Sonata in B flat, D.960.

Interpretation
A *da capo* of the minuet or scherzo is always intended after a trio, even when unmarked; but this time the repeats should be omitted. In some of Schubert's posthumously published works, e.g. the isolated Scherzos in B flat and D flat,

D.593, and the Allegretto in C minor, D.915, the repeats are printed in full. It seems certain, however, that this was merely a publisher's dodge to increase the number of pages in the original edition; so the two groups of duplicated bars in the recapitulation should be cut out in performance.

In simple RONDO FORM two or more episodes, generally in contrasted keys, separate statements of the main theme in the tonic: A B A C . . . A. More complex types often incorporate elements of sonata-form, as in the 2nd movement of Mozart's Sonata in C, K.545, where the C section is replaced by a development:

$$\textit{Key: } I \quad V \quad I \textit{ various} \qquad I$$
$$\text{A B A devel. } \overbrace{\text{A Coda;}}$$

or in the concerto-like finale of his Sonata in B flat, K.333:

$$\textit{Key: } I \quad V \quad I \quad \textit{vi} \quad \textit{IV} \qquad I$$
$$\text{A B A C D } \overbrace{\text{A B Cadenza A.}}$$

The possible varieties are almost endless, but in all rondos the A section appears at least three times.

VARIATIONS in a slow movement are invariably of the melodic type, and are unlikely to stray far from a single basic tempo (but see Chapter 3, Tempo: under Classical, p. 46). In a finale, or an isolated set of variations, more changes of tempo may be expected; but since these will be marked in the score they need cause no difficulty. The penultimate variation in such a set is often in a slow tempo, and is followed by a quick variation and coda in which both the harmonic range and phrase structure of the theme are considerably expanded. This underlines the feeling of finality by enlarging the time-scale.

Haydn was specially fond of variations on twin themes, one major and the other minor. Examples can be seen in the Minuet-finale of the Sonata in E, Hob.XVI/22, in the 1st movement of the Sonata in G, Hob.XVI/40, and on a much larger scale, in the superb Variations in F minor, Hob.XVII/6.

The Classical counterpart of Bach's 'Goldberg' Variations is Beethoven's monumental set of 'Diabelli' Variations, Op. 120.

ROMANTIC

Composers of the Romantic period also used sonata-form, but less frequently than their predecessors and sometimes with a slight feeling of constraint. (Brahms was exceptional in finding the Classical forms wholly congenial, though he wrote no solo sonatas after his early, and not altogether typical Op. 1, 2, and 5.) A promising development that had been foreshadowed in Schubert's 'Wanderer' Fantasia, D.760, and piano duet Fantasia in F minor, D.940, was the single-movement sonata combining many of the essential elements of a three- or four-movement work. Liszt's Sonata in B minor, S.178, is a brilliantly successful example; yet curiously enough it was never matched by another solo work of comparable stature.

More in keeping with the mood of the period were collections of pieces of some distinctive type, such as Mendelssohn's 'Songs without Words' (song imitations), Chopin's waltzes, mazurkas, and polonaises (idealized dances), and Schumann's 'Kinderscenen', 'Carnaval', and 'Kreisleriana' (illustrative or character pieces); or works with less evocative titles like études, preludes, impromptus, ballades, intermezzos, capriccios, rhapsodies, etc. Such movements have no prescribed forms, but, as before, their structures may be defined for purposes of study by marking their themes and sections with letters. If this is done, it will be found more often than not that the form revealed is either identical with, or closely related to, one or other of those that have already been described.

Further Reading

(See the following in Suggestions for Further Reading, pp. 177 ff.)

Apel, Willi, *Geschichte der Orgel- und Klaviermusik bis 1700*.
Bach, J. S., *48 Preludes and Fugues*, ed. Tovey.
  The 'Goldberg' Variations, ed. Kirkpatrick.
Beethoven, L. van, *Pianoforte Sonatas*, ed. Tovey.
Davie, Cedric Thorpe, *Musical Structure and Design*.
Morris, R. O., *The Structure of Music*.
Tovey, Donald Francis, *A Companion to [Bach's] 'The Art of Fugue'*.
  Essays in Musical Analysis: Chamber Music.
  The Forms of Music.

3 Tempo

The first problem that confronts the student of pre-classical music is to determine its tempo. This has troubled others before him, for we read in the introduction to Purcell's *A Choice Collection of Lessons*, 1696, that there is 'nothing more difficult in musick then playing of true time'. As a step towards solving the problem it will be helpful to consider for a moment some aspects of musical notation that are now obsolete.

During the 16th and 17th centuries notation was passing through one of its periodical phases of transition. It was moving towards the present-day system, in which the relative value of notes remains constant (1 breve = 2 semibreves = 4 minims, etc.), a time-signature shows how many notes of a given denomination occur in a bar, and a tempo mark indicates the speed at which they should be played. At the same time it was moving away from the old barless proportional system, in which the relative values of notes did not remain fixed, but were indicated by means of various symbols, the forerunners of our time-signatures.

In the proportional system *c.* 1600 the various note-ratios were in theory shown by the following four symbols:

Ø	O	¢	C
1 breve = 3 semibreves = 9 minims	1 breve = 3 semibreves = 6 minims	1 breve = 2 semibreves = 6 minims	1 breve = 2 semibreves = 4 minims

The symbols denoted not only the metrical structure of a piece but also its approximate tempo, for the speed of a movement was settled by reference to the semibreve as a standard time-unit. Modifications of these standard speeds were accomplished by the use of further signs, e.g.:

𝕆 halved the note-values of **O**

℃ or Ɔ   „   „   „   „   „ **C**

𝕀   „   „   „   „   „ ℃

$\frac{2}{1}$ (*dupla*, diminution) meant   o = previous ♩

$\frac{1}{2}$ (*dupla*, augmentation) meant ♩ = previous o

$\frac{3}{1}$ or 31 (*tripla*, diminution) meant   o o o = previous o

$\frac{3}{2}$ or 3 $\left(\begin{array}{c}\textit{sesquialtera,}\\ \text{diminution}\end{array}\right)$ meant   o o o = previous o o

(It will be noticed that the symbols **C** and **℃** have survived in modern notation. The numerals, on the other hand, are unrelated to their apparent modern equivalents; for the modern time-signature $\frac{3}{2}$ means three-minims-to-a-bar, not three-in-the-place-of-two; and $\frac{2}{1}$ now means two-semibreves-to-a-bar, not semibreve-equals-previous-minim.)

In practice the use of the signs was extraordinarily muddled, and different sources often give different signs for the same piece of music. Those most frequently encountered in English keyboard MSS are: **C** and **℃** for simple and compound duple time; $\frac{𝕆}{3}$, **℃**, and $\frac{℃}{3}$ for simple triple time; and 3 for brisk triple time. 31 or 3 in conjunction with a symbol was commonly used for a moderate triple time such as a galliard, while 3 standing alone indicated a quicker triple time such as a coranto or jig.

Another element of notation then in a state of transition was the unit of musical movement. It is a curious fact that the duration of notes tends to lengthen over the centuries—the breve, as its name implies, was originally short instead of very long. Hence we find that the normal unit of movement shifts every now and again to the next lower note-value. At the time of the virginalists, for example, it was hovering between the minim and its present-day value of a crotchet, as can be seen even within a single collection such as *Parthenia*, c. 1612/13, where four of the five pavans require a beat of c. 80 to the crotchet, whereas the fifth (No. 10, Bull's 'Pavana: St Thomas, wake!') requires the same beat to a minim.

It is essential to remember this gradual change when reading music of the 16th and 17th centuries in its original notation, otherwise there is a danger of playing it far too slowly. In an effort to avoid the risk many modern editors halve or quarter the original note-values; but this can be equally misleading, for if the notes of a German tablature book are quartered (as in Merian's edition; see under Anthologies, pp. 183 ff.), or those of a virginalist's coranto halved, they generally look much too fast. The player should therefore try to find editions that preserve the original note-values, and accustom himself to interpreting these correctly.

As to the actual time-value of the unit of movement: Mersenne in 1636, Christopher Simpson in 1665, and several later writers equated it with the human pulse, which means roughly 80 (see the pavans mentioned above). But it would be a mistake to expect all music to fit unfailingly into such a pre-ordained strait-jacket, however convenient it might be to the theorist; so we must in practice allow the unit to vary somewhat.

By the end of the 17th century time-signatures had taken the place of mensural signs; and at first they too had connotations of tempo. Purcell's *A Choice Collection of Lessons*, already mentioned, gives an explanation of their significance which may be tabulated thus:

Tempi as given in Purcell's
'A Choice Collection of Lessons', 1696

Common Time

C = 4 crotchets in a bar: a very slow movement

₵ = 4 crotchets in a bar: a little faster

Ↄ† = 4 crotchets in a bar: a brisk and airy time

Triple Time

$\frac{3}{2}$ = 3 minims in a bar: played very slow

31 = 3 crotchets in a bar: played slow

3 = 3 crotchets in a bar: played faster

$\frac{6}{4}$ = 6 crotchets in a bar: for brisk tunes like jigs and passpieds

† Misprinted as **Ɵ** in the original.

These signs do not always provide as much help in determining tempi as we might wish, for composers used them almost as inconsistently as the mensural signs. In Purcell's Suites, printed in the same volume, we find $\frac{3}{2}$ ('a very slow movement') used for a brisk hornpipe; and ₵ applied to an alman marked 'very slow', which clearly requires the sign **C**. (A confusion between **C** and ₵ is quite common, and the two signs will even be found in different instrumental parts of the same ensemble piece.)

On leaving English music we find that the problems of tempo begin to clarify slightly. The French harpsichord composers often prefixed their pieces with words such as Tenderly, Gaily, Quickly, or Slowly, sometimes implying a speed through a mood, and sometimes stating the speed directly. At times, however, these directions are merely intended as a warning or qualification: as for example in some of d'Anglebert's Gavottes, where the word *lentement* (slowly) does not mean that the piece should sound slow, but that the normal beat for a gavotte here applies to the quaver instead of the more usual crotchet or minim.

At about the same time, several French theorists began to measure dance tempi with primitive types of metronomes. From the writings of Michel L'Affilard (1694), L. L. Pajot (1732), J. A. La Chapelle (1737), and H. L. Choquel (1759) we may deduce the following speeds for some of the more important dances of the period:

	MM†	
Allemande	120	for each of 2 beats per bar
Courante	82–90	3
Gavotte	98–152	2
Gigue	104–120	2
Menuet	70–80	1
Rigaudon	116–152	2
Sarabande	63–80	3
Tambourin	176	2

Two points about this table must, however, be remembered. Firstly, the notation of the French harpsichordists often requires the beat to apply not to

† MM = Maelzel's Metronome (see under Classical and Romantic: Metronome marks, below).

half-bars (minims) but to crotchets, and sometimes even to quavers as we have seen from the gavottes of d'Anglebert. And secondly, the tempi were judged by the straightforward dances of the stage or ballroom, and therefore sometimes require to be slower for the richly elaborated movements of the harpsichordists. Generally speaking, it will be found that the beat remains more or less within the limits shown for the allemande, courante, gavotte, and sarabande, though not necessarily the number of beats per bar; while for the rigaudon and tambourin it will have to be somewhat slower, and for the gigue and menuet considerably slower.

It is also useful to remember that the tempo of dance movements tends to slow down over the years. For example, the sarabande was quick enough in Purcell's day to make a satisfactory finish to a Suite, whereas for Bach it was essentially a slow movement.

The familiar Italian tempo marks also began life as descriptions of mood, for the literal meaning of *allegro* is 'cheerful', while *adagio* means 'gently, at ease'; but by the mid-18th century they had already acquired most of the meanings we know today. J. J. Quantz in 1752 relates tempi to pulse-beats, like Mersenne and Simpson a hundred years earlier, and gives definitions which in terms of the metronome may be tabulated thus:

Speeds given by Quantz, 1752, for
Italian tempo-marks in Common-time

Presto, Allegro assai	♩ = 160
Vivace, Allegro, Allegro moderato	♩ = 120
Allegretto	♩ = 80
Adagio cantabile	♪ = 80
Adagio assai	♪ = 40

Like the earlier definitions, these will be found too restricted in practice; nevertheless, they are interesting from a comparative point of view and as very rough approximations.

With all questions of tempo the most important point is that the player should take into consideration the prevailing texture and movement of the music. A piece that is full of demi-semiquavers or very complicated ornamentation, or one that has harmonic shifts on every quaver, is likely to require a comparatively slow crotchet; while a piece that has no note smaller than a quaver, little ornamentation, and a change of harmony only once every minim, will need a crotchet that is comparatively quick. All such relevant factors must be weighed together and balanced with what is known or may be deduced of the form, character, and mood of the piece concerned. Then, as the player experiments with different tempi, he will at one point find that the rhythmic detail suddenly slips into focus, as it were, with what he conceives to be the mood of the piece. When this occurs he may feel tolerably certain that he has found the correct basic tempo of the movement concerned.

With regard to consistency of tempo within a single movement: the remarks already made concerning the interpretation of various forms should be borne in mind (see Chapter 2, pp. 13 ff.). It will be remembered that an important factor is the *type* of music involved. In forms that are free, such as improvisatory preludes and toccatas, the tempo will tend to be free; in sectional works, such as canzonas including more than a single time-signature, certain toccatas, and even some sets of variations, there may be changes of tempo between one section and another; and in the stricter, more self-contained forms, such as dances and fugues, the tempo is likely to remain basically unchanged. Borderline cases will often occur, of course, and for these the player must rely on his own common sense and musical instinct.

(Chapter 2, pp. 28 ff., includes information concerning the tempo of various dances.)

CLASSICAL AND ROMANTIC

From the mid 18th century onwards composers marked tempi with increasing care, and generally (like Quantz) in Italian, the *lingua franca* of music. The more important indications used for main sections are the following, in order of increasing speed: *Largo*, broad; *Lento*, slow; *Adagio*, slow; *Andante* (literally, 'walking'), slowish, but with movement; *Andantino* ('a little Andante'), ambiguous, but generally implying *quicker* than Andante; *Moderato*, moderate; *Allegretto* ('a little Allegro'), *slower* than Allegro; *Allegro*, quick; *Presto*, very quick; *Prestissimo*, as quick as possible. For smaller, local variations within these limits the commonest indications are: *ritardando* (*rit.*) or *rallentando* (*rall.*), getting slower; *accelerando* (*accel.*), getting quicker; with *a tempo* to show a return to the prevailing speed.

Many necessary tempo changes still remain unmarked, however, and it is up to the player to discover where they are required. The commonest are small, local variations (*rit.*, *accel.*, *a tempo*, etc.) which may be described as various types of *rubato* (see below, pp. 47 ff.). But sometimes in classical music, and more often in romantic, important sectional changes have not been indicated.

The typical large-scale forms of the classical period—e.g. the movements of a sonata or symphony—were usually conceived in a uniform tempo, apart from the small local changes already mentioned. It is therefore generally a mistake to play one section of a movement at a different tempo from that of another. For example, in the opening *Allegro con brio* of Beethoven's 'Waldstein' Sonata, Op. 53, small local variations of tempo may be in place, but the slowing down of its second subject (b. 35) to what Tovey dubs an *Andante religioso* is not. Nor is it either musical or logical to play the opening of the 'Appassionata' Sonata, Op. 57, at an entirely different speed from its recapitulation (b. 135), merely because the latter happens to have an added quaver accompaniment.

A basically uniform tempo—or at least the *impression* of a uniform tempo —should therefore be aimed at in classical music. Exceptions to the rule are most likely to occur in sets of variations, since these are in themselves sectional and at times contain abrupt changes of mood. An isolated minor variation in a major context, for instance, may imply so great an emotional contrast that it must be accommodated by some relaxation of tempo; and similar adjustments may be required elsewhere.

A subtle and unexpected type of tempo change is needed in certain rhythmically cumulative variations. In the slow movement of the 'Appassionata' Sonata, for example, where the theme is mainly in crotchets and the three variations are successively in quavers, semiquavers, and demi-semiquavers, it will be found that no single tempo fits both theme and third variation. This is not because of the difficulty experienced in some virginals music of playing sixteen demi-semiquavers in the time of one crotchet, it is for precisely the opposite reason: here there is too much time for the demi-semiquavers, for a curious aural illusion at times makes slow music sound less slow, and quick music less quick, than it is in fact being played. Hence if we want to give the *impression* of a uniform tempo in this movement, the speed must be increased very slightly with each succeeding variation—much as an ancient Greek architect made the lines of his buildings slightly curved in order to give an effect of straightness. Such progressive tempo changes are by no means always necessary in cumulative variations: they are, indeed, only likely to occur when the theme itself is on the slow side.

Some of Schubert's sonata-form movements, unlike those of Beethoven and earlier classical composers, require different tempi to suit the sharply contrasted moods of their themes. In the Sonata in A minor, Op. 42 (D. 845), it is impossible to find one tempo that makes sense of both the opening subject and its pendant (b. 26), for either the first will sound too fast or the second too slow. Here, and throughout the movement, two slightly different tempi seem to be intended. It is up to the player, therefore, to preserve the sense of continuity by making the changes as unobtrusive as possible. Where a musical link exists, a gradual transition can often be made from one tempo to the other, as in bb. 10–20, where a slight accelerando will carry the listener imperceptibly from the relaxed mood of the opening to the more urgent mood of b. 26. If there are no links, as in the last dozen bars of the exposition, the changes will perforce be abrupt.

With the advent of romantic music tempi in general become more fluid than before. Sectional changes are more usual and local changes more exaggerated, and the two types even merge at times. Luckily for the performer, the sectional changes are generally clearly marked. Exceptions do occur, however; particularly in the Chopin mazurkas, whose rhythmic freedom is a legacy of their prototype, the Polish folksong-cum-dance. Some of the mazurkas require two distinct tempi, like the Schubert A minor Sonata; but here the difference between the two is likely to be greater than in the earlier work. As before, the player will generally find that the presence of a musical link implies a gradual transition from one tempo to the other, while the absence of a link implies an abrupt change. Examples of both will be found in the Mazurka in C sharp minor, Op. 50/3 (*S & I* IV, p. 28), which also contains an interesting combination of tempo-change and rubato, very typical of Chopin. In it, there is a gradual shift from the slower to the quicker of two tempi, followed by a gradual return to the original speed, the whole forming what might be called a 'rhythmic arch' in bb. 9–16.

Not all of Chopin's mazurkas require sectional tempo changes. The Mazurka in A flat Op. 24/3 (*S & I* IV, p. 26) is one of the many that has a single basic tempo throughout; though small local variations are of course still essential to the life of the music.

RUBATO

During the earlier part of the present century the true nature of rubato was hotly disputed: did it, through an exact balance of *rit.* and *accel.*, leave the basic pulse unchanged in the long run? or did it radically disrupt the pulse? The answer is that it does both, for there are two different kinds of rubato: melodic and structural.

In *melodic rubato* the accompaniment keeps strict time, while the melody follows the minutely freer dictates of 'vocal' expressiveness. The two rhythms coincide at structurally important points in the bar or phrase, and thus the basic pulse remains intact.

Early examples of one type of this rubato are found in the *notes inégales* of the French harpsichordists; and Mozart later referred to another aspect of it when he wrote to his father in October 1777:

> Everyone is amazed that I can always keep strict time. What these people cannot grasp is that in tempo rubato in an Adagio, the left hand should go on playing in strict time. With them the left hand always follows suit.

Descriptions of melodic rubato (though under different names) appear in treatises from the early 18th century onwards, including those of Couperin (1717), Tosi (1723), Quantz (1752), C. P. E. Bach (1753), and Leopold Mozart (1756). In the 19th century it was taught by Chopin, who told his pupils that the singing hand may deviate, but the accompaniment must keep time. And today it is heard continually in the melodic anticipations and delays of jazz musicians. It is, indeed, so natural a part of any music founded on a vocal style, that it is likely to have been used, if not defined, long before the 18th century.

In *structural rubato*, the second of our two types, melody and accompaniment deviate from strict tempo simultaneously. This means that no exact balance of *rit.* and *accel.* is needed to keep the hands together; and since such a balance is unlikely to be achieved by accident, there is almost bound to be a change in the basic pulse.

This type of rubato will be much more familiar to the player than the other, for he uses it whenever he obeys a composer's direction *rit. - - - a tempo*, or makes the smallest unmarked *rit.* or *accel.* on his own initiative. It was equally familiar to early writers, one of the first to mention it being Frescobaldi in the prefaces to his *Toccate e Partite*, 1614–15, and *Il primo libro di capricci*, 1624. (See Chapter 2, section 5, pp. 21 ff., under Preludes and Toccatas.) It too is such a natural part of any music founded on a vocal style that we can safely assume it was known and practised from the earliest times.

How, then, should the player of today use these two different types of rubato in his interpretation of music of different periods? No detailed answer can be given to this question, for the convincing use of rubato depends more on feeling and instinct than on rule. Nevertheless, the following hints may provide some rough guidance:

1. Rubato of one kind or another is natural to most music, except when its appeal is predominantly rhythmic (marches, quick dances, etc.).

2. Melodic rubato, in which the rhythm of the accompaniment is strictly maintained while the melody deviates from it, is a type of 'vocal' expressiveness. Only very small rhythmic deviations are involved, and it is more likely to be needed in slow music than in fast.

3. Structural rubato, in which melody and accompaniment together deviate from strict tempo, is characteristic of almost all types of music, except the purely rhythmical. It is used not only for its expressive value, but also at times to help define phrasing and structure. It can be anything from a scarcely perceptible delay to a broad *rit.* or *accel.*, or *rit.* and *accel.* combined.

4. The *degree* of rubato used contributes more than anything else to the rightness or wrongness of its effect.

5. Romantic types of music require more pronounced rubato than classical. Hence music of the 19th century is likely on the whole to require greater rhythmic freedom than that of the 18th.

6. Within this broad classification, a romantically minded composer will require a more pronounced rubato than one who is classically minded. Thus, moving backwards in time, Schumann requires more freedom than Brahms, Chopin more than Mendelssohn, Schubert more than Beethoven, W. F. Bach more than his brother Johann Christian, and Froberger more than Couperin.

7. The freer forms are likely to require a corresponding freedom of rhythm, while the stricter forms generally (but not invariably) require less freedom.

8. No matter how extreme a rubato is used, the player must always take the greatest care never to lose sight of the basic structure of the music.

METRONOME MARKS

Metronome marks would seem at first sight to solve every problem concerning the notation and interpretation of tempi; yet in practice they often pose almost as many questions as they answer.

The modern metronome was perfected in 1816 by a German mechanician named Johann Nepomuk Maelzel (1772–1838). Beethoven was at first greatly interested in the device. He had welcomed its immediate forerunner in 1812 with a short Canon ('Ta, ta, ta . . .', WoO 162 in Kinsky's catalogue), afterwards used as the opening theme of the Allegretto movement of the Eighth Symphony; and in 1817 and 1819 he issued two small booklets containing metronome markings for the eleven string quartets and eight symphonies that he had already published. He also included metronome marks in several subsequent works as they appeared, notably the 'Hammerklavier' Sonata, Op. 106, and the Ninth Symphony, Op. 125. Significantly enough, however, there are none in the last six string quartets and the last three piano sonatas—a fact which suggests that Beethoven, like Wagner a quarter of a century later, eventually lost faith in the usefulness of the metronome.

There are several possible reasons for such a change of attitude. Firstly, metronome marks may suggest to the performer that tempi are absolute, whereas experience shows that they depend to a certain extent on variable factors, such as acoustical conditions, the instrument used, etc. Secondly, a composer, unless he checks and re-checks his markings, can all too easily put down a figure that seriously misrepresents his true intentions, particularly if he attempts (as Beethoven must have done) to mark a large number of works in a short space of time. Thirdly, it is sometimes impossible to find a single metronome mark that makes sense of a whole movement, or even of a section of a movement. And lastly, metronomes in themselves are often inaccurate: for example, two machines set at the same figure will rarely tick at exactly the same speed; while even a single machine set at (say) 50 will hardly ever tick just half as slowly as when set at 100.

It seems likely that some or all of these reasons must have accounted not only for Beethoven's ultimate rejection of the metronome, but also for Brahms's complete avoidance of it. Other composers were less consistent: sometimes they included metronome marks in their scores and sometimes not. When a figure is given, it *may* supply a valuable clue to the composer's intentions. On the other hand, it may equally well be totally misleading.

Schumann was particularly unreliable in this respect. In his *Kinderscenen*, Op. 15, for example, it is often quite impossible to reconcile the metronome marks with the moods implied by the titles. (There are no normal tempo indications.) Thus in the very first piece, 'Of Strange Lands and Peoples', a speed of $\quarternote = 108$ seems considerably too quick and matter-of-fact to convey the intended atmosphere of 'once-upon-a-time'; while 'A Curious Story', which follows, becomes flat-footed and humourless if played as slowly as

Schumann's ♩ = 112. Two later markings are even more unconvincing. No. 7, 'Dreaming', would sound far from dream-like if played as quickly as ♩ = 100; and in No. 10, 'Almost too serious', ♩ = 69 seems so absurdly fast as to make one think that it must be a misprint for ♪ = 69. Most of the remaining metronome marks in *Kinderscenen*, and many of those in Schumann's other works seem equally improbable; and it is significant that after his death his widow, Clara Schumann, altered a great number of them in the complete edition she edited. If the original figures were consistently either too fast or too slow it would be less puzzling, for then one would assume that Schumann's machine had been wrongly regulated; but as we have already seen, this is not so. Such apparently capricious markings are hard to account for, unless the explanation is as simple as that given by a present-day composer concerning his own works. When asked about his somewhat unexpected metronome markings he replied, 'Are they wrong? I never thought of testing them with a machine.'

With this startling admission in mind, even if for no other reason, the player will understand that it is not *always* wise to follow metronome marks literally. What then should be done about them?

The safest rule is to assume that any metronome mark is worth noting, if the composer has put it there. It should always be tried out—not simply ignored, as so often happens. Then, if it is found to illuminate and make sense of the music, it should be accepted as an indication of the basic tempo of the movement or section of a movement, rather than as a speed from which the player may never deviate by a hair's-breadth. On the other hand, if the music sounds persistently 'wrong' or uncomfortable at the speed indicated, the player must feel free to experiment with different tempi: slightly slower or faster in the first instance, to allow for small differences between metronomes; then, if need be, at tempi that are considerably faster or slower, to allow for Schumann-like quirks. As suggested earlier, at some point in this process the player will find that the rhythmic detail of the music suddenly slips into focus with its mood; and when this happens, he may feel tolerably certain that he has found the correct basic tempo of the movement or section concerned.

Metronomic rhythm is rarely an ideal to be aimed at in performance, except in cases such as quick dances and marches. Almost every other kind of music— and romantic music in particular—'breathes' in a way that is altogether foreign to a machine. In spite of this, the metronome can be exceedingly useful at times for purposes of practice. It may never allow the player sufficient time for the *rits.* and more subtle kinds of rubato that he would normally make; but it will show him, generally to his pain and surprise, that he often unconsciously hurries a crescendo, drags a diminuendo, clips the ends of runs, and so on. Not all of these tendencies are invariably out of place; but the player should be aware of them, and only indulge them when he intends to do so, otherwise his performance will become flaccid and uncontrolled.

Further Reading

(See the following in Suggestions for Further Reading, pp. 177 ff.)

Badura-Skoda, Eva and Paul, *Interpreting Mozart on the Keyboard.*
Borrel, Eugène, *L'Interpretation de la musique française.*
Dolmetsch, Arnold, *The Interpretation of Music . . .*
Donington, Robert, *The Interpretation of Early Music.*
Grove's Dictionary, under Expression, Notation.
Harding, Rosamond E. M., *Origins of Musical Time and Expression*
Sachs, Kurt, *Rhythm and Tempo.*

4 Phrasing and Articulation

PRE-CLASSICAL

Problems of phrasing and articulation might at first sight seem less important than those of tempo; yet, if anything, the reverse is true. Phrasing, though so rarely marked in early scores, is the breath and life of music, and a performance that lacks it is as meaningless as unpunctuated speech. It is therefore essential for a player to learn to phrase and articulate an unmarked score idiomatically.

As the terms are often loosely used, it may be as well to begin with three definitions. In the following discussion a *phrase* is taken to be a natural musical division comparable to a sentence of speech; hence *phrasing* is concerned with showing these divisions, both short and long, and their relationship one with another. *Articulation*, on the other hand, is a subsidiary of phrasing, and is concerned with whether a note is joined to its neighbour or neighbours, or is in some degree detached.

PHRASING

Musical phrases, like spoken sentences, are defined by being separated from one another by 'breaths' of varying length, corresponding roughly to the effect of commas, semi-colons, full-stops, etc. These minute silences are made, generally without disturbing the time-scheme, by shortening the last note of a phrase; but when a more marked break is required, it may be also necessary occasionally—particularly in more romantic types of music—to lengthen the bar by a fraction, or even to make a tiny *rit*. Such breaks are infinitesimal, and much of the art of phrasing lies in the subtlety with which they are differentiated and executed.

To discover the phrasing of an unmarked and unfamiliar work, the player should begin by reading it through as best he may. He should then turn back to the beginning and play as far as the first obvious halting place, such as a specially strong cadence, a cadence preceding a new musical idea, or a double bar. Having established this initial paragraph, he should then proceed to break it down into its constituent sections and phrases, which he will find are generally rounded off by cadences of varying strength. Finally, with these musical divisions clearly in his head, or marked in pencil on the score, he should ask himself two questions: (a) which are the more important and which are the less important breaks between phrases? and (b) where is the climax of the whole paragraph?—that is, the point towards which the tension mounts and away from which it slackens.

Having analysed the first paragraph in this way, he should pass on to the second and treat it similarly. And so on with the rest of the work; always relating each new paragraph to those that have gone before, so that the whole is kept in correct perspective and the main climax of the work is clearly differentiated from the less important climaxes.

As an example of this approach it will be helpful to consider for a moment a short piece by Byrd from *Parthenia*, 1612/13:

Ex. 14 William Byrd, Galiardo

After reading the piece through, without bothering about ornamentation or minor details the player would start again at the beginning and play probably to the end of b.8, where there is both a strong cadence and a double bar. On returning once more to the beginning, he would find that this initial paragraph is made up of the following three phrases:

1. b.1 to the 3rd crotchet of b.4
2. 4th crotchet of b.4 to the 3rd crotchet of b.6
3. 4th crotchet of b.6 to the end of b.8

Considering their relationship, he would find that the most important break (the equivalent of a full-stop) comes at the end of the third; that there is a less important break (a semi-colon) at the end of the first; and a still less important one (a comma) at the end of the second. He would also find that the climax of the paragraph coincides with the melodic climax on the 3rd crotchet of b.7.

Having established the shape of this first paragraph, the player would then pass on to the second—which also happens to be the last—and analyse it similarly. (It contains three phrases: 1. b.9 to the 3rd crotchet of b.12; 2. 4th crotchet of b.12 to the 3rd crotchet of b.13; 3. 4th crotchet of b.13 to the end of b.16.) Here however he would find that the climax is harmonic rather than melodic. It occurs on the 1st crotchet of b.15; and since it is more intense than that of the previous paragraph, it also forms the climax of the whole piece.

Phrase-analysis of this kind not only shows the performer where the music 'breathes', it also provides him with a key to one of the most important forms of contrast available to a composer: the use of varying phrase-lengths. At first sight Byrd's Galiardo might seem a rather square little piece consisting of sixteen bars divided into two equal halves. Yet analysis shows—and the player must make this clear to the listener—that it is far from square, since it is made up of the following unexpected sequence of bars: $3\frac{1}{2}$, 2, $2\frac{1}{2}$: $3\frac{1}{2}$, 1, $3\frac{1}{2}$.

The player must also be on the lookout for the less straightforward types of phrase that either overlap or dovetail.

Overlapping phrases occur most frequently between different voices in contrapuntal textures, where the entries of the voices are usually 'staggered' to a greater or lesser degree. Examples can be found in bb.5–8 of the same Byrd Galiardo, where the l.h. echoes the r.h. at the distance of a bar. Such overlaps are characteristic of all contrapuntal music, whether imitation is present or not; so much so, indeed, that the student should always question his phrasing of counterpoint if he finds, at points other than cadences, that phrases in different voices end simultaneously.

In *Dovetailed phrases* a single note provides both the end of one phrase and the beginning of the next. There are several in the Prelude to Purcell's Suite No. 2 in G minor (*S & I* I, p. 36): e.g. the first r.h. semiquaver D in b.11, and the first r.h. B flat in b.20. Such joins sometimes require a fraction of extra time in performance—as for example at the end of b.10 of the Prelude, where the structurally important cadence will sound perfunctory if played strictly in time:

Ex. 15 Henry Purcell, Prelude from Suite No. 2
  (CE I, p. 2; *S & I* I, p. 36) *dovetail*

As pointed out earlier (see Chapter 2, Musical Types and Forms: under Pre-Classical, Dances, p. 30), a characteristic feature of the cadences in a French courante is the type of cross-rhythm known as *hemiola*: i.e. | ♩ ♩ ♩ | in a context of | ♩. ♩. |. It also occurs elsewhere and often indicates an important cadence. Handel was particularly fond of the less obvious form

which was sometimes written

ARTICULATION

Once the length of a phrase has been found, the next thing to decide is how it should be articulated: i.e. which of its notes shall be separated (and to what extent), and which joined to its neighbour or neighbours.

From surviving examples of early keyboard fingering it is clear that the music of the 16th, 17th, and early 18th centuries was broken up in performance into much smaller units than is customary with late 18th- and 19th-century music. (See Chapter 5: Fingering.) Players originally relied mainly on the middle three fingers of each hand, passing the long 3rd finger over the 4th in r.h. ascending scales and over the 2nd in descending ones (vice versa in the l.h.), and the 5th finger and thumb were used far less frequently than in present-day fingering. As a result, music was generally less smoothly articulated than it would be today—though of course a grave or stately mood would have called for more sustained treatment, e.g. in Byrd's 'Pavana: The Earle of Salisbury', or Gibbon's 'Fantazia of Foure Parts', both from *Parthenia* (*S & I* I, pp. 24 & 30 respectively).

The type of broken articulation required by much early music can be seen from the Byrd Galiardo already mentioned. If its first half were played legato, as is perfectly possible with modern fingering, it would sound airless, flat and dull. But when its opening phrase is articulated in some such way as

the dance-like character of the piece immediately becomes apparent, and the lively imitation between the voices stands out clearly.

This 'characterization' of themes is one of the most important functions of articulation in the performance of early music, for it brings out their inherent life and enables the most involved contrapuntal textures to remain transparent. Another of its functions is to define the smaller units out of which passage-work is built.

Long legato stretches of quickly moving notes, so characteristic of 19th-century composers such as Chopin and Liszt, are foreign to harpsichord music and reduce it to the level of a Czerny exercise. For an idiomatic performance, the player must always be aware of the smaller patterns that underlie the figuration, and aim to show these by means of subtle articulation, while preserving at the same time the all-important overall line. Indeed, to be aware of the sub-divisions is almost sufficient, for if they are over-emphasized the long line will disappear.

For example, in Farnaby's 'Tell mee Daphne':

Ex. 16 Giles Farnaby, 'Tell mee Daphne'
    (*FWVB* II, p. 446; *S & I* I, p. 28)

the semiquavers in bb.9–10 must be felt to consist of four-note
groups, beginning on the second semiquaver of each beat. The unbroken line
of the first half of b.11 then comes as a welcome contrast, followed by the unexpected break in the second half of the bar between the two l.h. Ds. Upbeat
articulation is resumed in b.12, first of all in groups of eight semiquavers and
then in groups of four, and is continued until the end of strain 2, apart from a
further refreshing contrast of four pairs of semiquavers in the first half of b.15.

In order to make such subtleties of articulation clear, it is almost always necessary to play quickly-moving early music at a noticeably slower tempo than would be natural to passage-work of the 19th century. The notes must be allowed time to breathe and establish their individuality, as it were, and never herded into anonymous groups. This rule applies equally strongly to the music of baroque composers such as Couperin and Bach, even though the increasing use of the thumb and fifth finger was beginning to bring greater speeds within the players' reach, as can be seen from some of the startlingly brilliant sonatas of Scarlatti.

But even when the fundamental importance of articulation is recognized and accepted, the student is still faced with the problem of how he shall decide its details.

Perhaps the best approach to finding the articulation of a phrase in an unmarked score is to sing, hum, or whistle it. This may not provide the final answer; but it leads in the right direction, for it shows the melodic contour, the climax of the phrase, the notes that form indivisible musical groups, and the places where natural breaks occur. Next the student might imagine how the phrase would be bowed by a string player, and in particular just how detached each individual non-legato note would be. He should then think of the harmonic aspect, and make sure that both the basic harmony and the progressions underlying the melodic decoration are supported and not contradicted by the articulation. For example, in the following Gavott by Blow:

Ex. 17 John Blow, Gavott (*S & I* I, p. 35)

the r.h. part taken by itself might suggest that a new sub-phrase begins on the 4th beat E of b.2; yet a glance at the bass shows that in fact the E belongs to the preceding F since it supplies its resolution, and that therefore the two notes must be slurred together.

By analogy with vocal music it will often be found that stepwise movement suggests legato, particularly if the steps are chromatic; while jumps (other than arpeggios, which are often merely broken chords) suggest staccato. Hence a leap interrupting stepwise movement is likely to imply a break in legato. This is of course only the roughest of generalizations, which is often invalidated by other considerations.

True syncopations—that is, misplaced accents and not simply resolutions of appoggiaturas—can generally be treated fairly consistently. As one of the clearest ways to accent a note (the only way, indeed, on the organ) is to shorten the one before it, the note preceding a syncopation usually tends to be more or less staccato.

Two slightly misleading types of notation, both concerned with articulation, must be remembered. In one, a single line is written as though it were in two parts; in the other, on the contrary, two sustained parts are written as though they were a single line. In Bach's F minor Prelude from Book I of the '48' the r.h. is notated thus:

But this does not mean, as it would in later piano music, that the notes with crotchet stems should be made to stand out as a separate melodic part. A moment's experiment on a harpsichord will show that the melody is contained in the semiquaver line, and that the crotchets are held down merely to enrich the harmonic background. The same notation is also used occasionally to show that all the notes relevant to the harmony should be sustained, and not only those that are marked.

Almost the opposite situation is found in passages such as the following from the Allemande of Bach's French Suite No. 4 in E flat:

Here a contemporary performer would almost certainly have played *molto tenuto*, as a contrast to the true single line of the r.h. in the preceding $2\frac{1}{2}$ bars:

This type of tenuto touch is immensely important in the performance of early keyboard music, for it provides tonal and textural contrast, adds warmth of sound, and virtually takes the place of the sustaining pedal of a modern piano. It must be used with discretion, however, and never with notes that are extraneous to the harmony.

The 18th century saw the increasing use of slurs, borrowed from string bowing, to indicate legato. (François Couperin devised the form ⌞____⌟ to differentiate a slur from a tie.) The sign for a staccato was either a small stroke (') or a wedge (') as staccato dots were not introduced until later in the century. (For the special meaning of slurs, dots, and staccato dashes in French harpsichord music, see Chapter 6, Rhythmic Conventions: under *Notes Inégales*, p. 102.)

FURTHER HINTS

1. An excess of legato in performance produces opaque stodginess, and too much staccato makes for a restless lack of continuity. Some pieces demand more legato and less staccato than others, and vice versa; but on the whole the two should be fairly evenly balanced.

2. The degree of staccato required is not always the same. It depends entirely on the context, and may be anything from the shortest staccatissimo to a portato that is only one stage removed from legato.

3. Look out for patterns of figuration and of phrase-length, and note particularly where they change.

4. Figurative patterns that match should have matching articulation: those that differ should have differing articulation.

5. 'Characterize' fugue subjects, counter-subjects, and episodes with suitably contrasted articulation, so that they may preserve their identity.

6. In pre-classical music, up-beat phrasing is more usual than on-the-beat phrasing. When a piece or a paragraph begins with an up-beat, the phrasing thereafter tends to do likewise.

7. Since a cadence = repose, and a climax = tension, the climax of a paragraph is almost certain to be a chord other than the prevailing tonic.

8. A dissonance or suspension should not be separated from its resolution. There is, however, an exception to this rule. If the resolution is ornamental, with one or more notes interposed between it and the discord, a new phrase often begins on the first note of the ornamental resolution.

CLASSICAL

Though rare in the pre-classical period, marks of phrasing and articulation were used increasingly after the mid-18th century. Nevertheless, some works remain wholly or partly unmarked, and here the player must be prepared to supply his own phrasing and articulation, basing them on the type of indications the composer concerned has used elsewhere. He may also find it helpful to bear in mind the general hints given above concerning pre-classical phrasing, though he will find that phrases in classical music do not habitually subdivide into such small units as those in the baroque period or earlier.

With music that has been marked by the composer, whether fully or only in part, the player should remember some differences between the notational conventions of the classical period and of today. These are concerned mainly with staccato signs, slurs, and the use of tenuto touch.

STACCATO DOTS, STROKES, AND WEDGES (·, ˈ, & ˈ)

A staccato was originally indicated, as we have seen, by either a short stroke (ˈ) or a wedge (ˈ). The two signs existed because a stroke is easier to write and a wedge easier to engrave.

Both Haydn and the youthful Mozart were in the habit of using a stroke to indicate a normal staccato, an accent, or a combination of the two; and of reserving dots, either slurred or unslurred, for mezzo-staccatos such as groups of repeated notes. Mozart later used dots with increasing freedom. He placed them not only over repeated notes, but also over all sorts of *leggiero* passages, including scales and upbeat figures of varying length. His stroke, on the other hand, retained its dual purpose of staccato and accent—at times it was purely accentual—and was also used as a more powerful contrast to the dot, generally, but not exclusively, in *forte* contexts. The difference between stroke and dot is usually clear in Mozart's autograph; but occasionally, since a quickly written dot can easily degenerate into a short stroke, it is difficult to tell which of the two was intended.

By the early 19th century the process of change had been carried a stage further. From Friedrich Starke's *Wiener Pianoforte Schule*, 1821, to which Beethoven contributed five of his Bagatelles, Op. 119, we learn that staccatos can be divided into three types: (1) a staccatissimo, indicated by a stroke [or wedge], where the note is held for only a quarter of its written value; (2) a normal staccato, indicated by a dot, where the note is held for half its value; and (3) a mezzo-staccato, indicated by ⌒·····, where the note is held for three-quarters of its value. It is not known whether Beethoven subscribed to these precise definitions, but he certainly differentiated between the stroke and the dot, for he used the two side by side as early as 1792 in his Sonata in E flat, Op. 7 (2nd movement, bb. 20 and 25); and towards the end of his life, in 1825, he wrote to the violinist Karl Holz, who was correcting string quartet parts for him: 'Where there is a dot above a note a dash must not be put instead, and vice versa—($\dot{r}$ $\dot{r}$ $\dot{r}$ and $\dot{r}$ $\dot{r}$ $\dot{r}$ are not identical).'

From the foregoing it can be seen that during the course of the 18th century the sign for a normal staccato was changing from the written stroke (') or printed wedge (') to the dot (·). Hence it should be remembered that in music of the early part of the 18th century the wedge was the exact equivalent of the dot of today, and not a staccatissimo. Later in the century the wedge implied either a staccato, an accent, or a combination of the two. (Schubert always intended it thus.) Finally, fairly early in the 19th century, the wedge became the staccatissimo that we know today.

It must also be remembered, however, that many late 19th- and 20th-century editions suppressed the wedge entirely and used only the dot. This is a regrettable and false simplification; for however difficult it may be at times to tell which of the two was intended in a MS, the difference between wedge (or stroke) and dot is real, and to ignore it is to deprive the player of an invaluable aid to interpretation.

Needless to say, the exact duration of any of these staccato marks must be judged, as in pre-classical works, more by the musical context than by mathematical definitions. Composers vary in their usage, not only from one another but from work to work. In the last resort, therefore, it is always the player's musical instinct that must decide the precise degree of staccato of any particular note. He will discover, for example, that a loud staccato chord tends to sound unpleasantly harsh unless fractionally longer than a quiet one. In a crescendo, therefore, staccato chords may need to get progressively, though infinitesimally, *less* staccato the louder they grow—unless a harsh effect is required.

A further point should be mentioned. Composers at times used staccato dots to indicate lightly accentuated notes in passage-work, as in the Beethoven Sonata in A flat, Op. 110, 1st movement, b.12 ff:

SLURS

A slur in early classical piano music can mean two different things. In the figure  it might imply that the last slurred note is non-legato: (an articulating slur); or, on the contrary, that it is legato: (a legato slur). This ambiguity arose from the fact that keyboard slurs were developed from string bow-marks, which are equally indefinite on this point, and depend for their interpretation, like slurs, on the context. In deciding which meaning should be attached to any particular slur, it will be helpful to remember the following points.

Articulating slurs are always short, and rarely include more than two or, at most, three notes. Generally they imply a stress on the first note, as well as the slight 'lift' or staccato on the last that has already been mentioned.

Legato slurs, like bow-marks, tend to stop just before barlines or strong beats; and they often divide a long legato line into smaller units, without implying any noticeable break, as can be seen from Beethoven's Bagatelle in E flat, Op. 126, No. 3:

Ex. 18 Beethoven, Bagatelle in E flat, Op. 126/3 (*S & I* III, p. 54)

Here the opening phrase is clearly one unbroken line until at least the second quaver of b.4; and it is quite likely that it should remain unbroken until the end of the first paragraph in b.16, for Beethoven has marked a slur across the expected phrase-ending in b.8.

At times, particularly in their later works, both Mozart and Beethoven ignored the barrier of the barline and made their legato slurs longer; but neither they nor Schubert ever entirely abandoned the early habit of treating them as though they were bow-marks.

TENUTO TOUCH

Tenuto touch—the holding down of notes for longer than their written value —is at times just as necessary in classical piano music as in earlier harpsichord works. A good instance is the opening of Mozart's Fantasia in D minor, K.397, where the broken chords in bb.1–6 would sound absurdly dry if they were not sustained until the end of the bar:

Ex. 19 Mozart, Fantasia in D minor, K. 397 (*S & I* III, p. 33)

Here the r.h. pedal could achieve a similar (though not identical) effect; but not in bb.7–8, where the topmost note in each half-bar is an appoggiatura which should *not* be sustained.

Often, for reasons of clarity or colour, it is preferable to sustain notes with the fingers rather than with the r.h. pedal, particularly in Alberti basses and kindred accompaniment figures. These should, of course, be played exactly as written whenever a brilliant, glittering, or light effect is required; but at other times it may be found helpful to introduce varying degrees of tenuto touch in order to obtain continually varying changes of colour and/or dynamics. The possibilities of variety are almost endless, so it is important to remember that this type of touch is part and parcel of the keyboard style of the period.

Further Reading

(See the following in Suggestions for Further Reading, pp. 177 ff.)

Badura-Skoda, Eva and Paul, *Interpreting Mozart on the Keyboard*.
Grove's Dictionary, under Phrasing.

5 Fingering

As pointed out in the previous chapter, early systems of keyboard fingering differed considerably from those in general use today. Whereas the modern systems minimize so far as possible the differences in length between the five digits, the earlier systems exploited them. Hence the thumb and fifth finger were used far less than today, and the middle three fingers far more. In addition, there was a tendency to associate 'good' (i.e. rhythmically strong) notes with the so-called 'good' fingers, and 'bad' notes with the 'bad'; but different authorities classified the fingers in different ways and the rule was often ignored.

The majority of players would now find it impractical to follow the various older systems, for that would mean unlearning their own. Nevertheless, a knowledge of the principles on which they were based is useful, for it provides an important clue to the type of articulation formerly in use.

In the following examples the various early notations used for fingering have all been normalized. When only one finger is indicated on an ornament, it *always* belongs to the main (i.e. printed) note,

hence .

EARLY FINGERING

In the early systems the thumb was rarely used as a pivot over which the fingers could pass either up or down the scale—and then virtually only in the left hand. Lateral movement of the hands was most often achieved by passing one of the middle fingers (usually the long 3rd) over one of its neighbours. Thus in the right hand the 3rd finger would be slipped over the 4th when ascending, and over the 2nd when descending; and in the left hand vice versa:

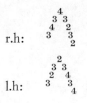

At times, however, the 2nd finger was shifted rather awkwardly over the 3rd in r.h. ascent and l.h. descent, to allow a 'good' finger to coincide with a 'good' note:

$$\text{r.h:}\ \ 2\ {\overset{\displaystyle 3}{\underset{\displaystyle 3}{\overset{2}{}}}}\qquad \text{l.h:}\ \ {\overset{\displaystyle 2}{\underset{\displaystyle 3}{\overset{3}{\underset{2}{}}}}}.$$

In 16th-century Germany and Italy the 'good' fingers were the 2nd & 4th, while elsewhere they were generally the 1st, 3rd, & 5th. The basic difference can be seen from the table in Ex. 20, which also shows how the more practical second classification gradually spread from England, via the Netherlands, to Northern Germany and the rest of Europe.

Ex. 20 Early Fingerings of Diatonic Scale Passages ('good' fingers in bold type)

	L.H. ascending	L.H. descending	R.H. ascending	R.H. descending
Buchner, c. 1520		2 3 2 3 2 3 2	2 3 2 3 2 3 4	4 3 2 3 2 3 2
Ammerbach, 1571	4 3 2 1 4 3 2	2 3 2 3 2 3 4	2 3 2 3 2 3 4	4 3 2 3 2 3 2
Diruta, 1593	4 3 2 3 2 3 2	2 3 2 3 2 3 4	2 3 4 3 4 3 4	4 3 2 3 2 3 2
Cabezón, 1578	4 3 2 1	1 2 3 4	3 4 3 4	3 2 3 2
English Virginalists	5 4 3 2 1 2 1	1 2 3 4 3 4 5	3 4 3 4 3 4 5	5 4 3 2 3 2 3
Sweelinck	5 4 3 2 1 2 / 5 4 3 [3 2] 1	1 2 3 2 3 4 / 1 2 3 1 2 3 4	2 3 4 3 4 5	{ 4 3 2 1 2 3 / 5 4 3 3 2 3 }
Scheidemann	{ 2 1 2 / 4 3 2 } [1] 2		3 4 3 4 5	5 4 3 2 3 2
Purcell, 1696	5 4 3 2 3 2 1	1 2 3 4 3 4 5	1 2 3 4 3 4 5	5 4 3 2 3 2 1
J. S. Bach, 1720	[5 4] 3 2 1 2 1	[1 2 1] 2 3 4 3 4 5	3 4 3 4 3 4 5	5 4 3 2 3 2 1
Nivers, 1665	4 3 2 1 2 1	{ 1 2 3 4 3 4 / 1 2 3 4 3 4 5 }	{ 2 3 4 3 4 / 1 2 3 4 3 4 }	{ 4 3 2 3 3 1 / 4 3 2 2 3 2 }
F. Couperin, 1716	5 4 3 [3 2] 1	1 2 3 4 3 4 / 1 2 3 4 3 5	1 2 3 4 { 3 4 / 2 3 }	5 4 3 2 3 2 1 / 5 4 3 3 2 2

The following examples show how the two systems were applied in more extended contexts:

'Good' 2nd & 4th Fingers

Ex. 21 Johannes Buchner, 'Quem terra, pontus' from *Fundamentum*, c. 1520 (the earliest known keyboard fingering).

If read literally some of the above fingerings would be impossible, even on a narrow-keyed 16th-century instrument: e.g. r.h. b.10, and l.h. bb.4, 5, 6, 8, & 12. Assuming that the manuscript is not inaccurate, one can only conclude that notes were sometimes held for less than their written value, or even omitted altogether if they duplicated the preceding note, as with the second C in l.h. b.4.

Ex. 22 Elias Nicolaus Ammerbach, *Orgel oder Instrument Tabulatur*, 1571

Though Ammerbach generally treated the 2nd & 4th fingers as 'good', he here substitutes the more convenient 3rd at every r.h. occurrence of the opening 4-note figure. Note the repetition of a finger on the r.h. 1st note of groups 3, 4, & 6.

'Good' 1st, 3rd, & 5th Fingers

Ex. 23 John Bull, Preludium [before 1599] (CE II, p. 134)

Almost identical fingering is found in three out of the four sources of this prelude. An alternative passage is shown in l.h. b.7.

Ex. 24 Orlando Gibbons, 'The Woods so Wild' (CE, p. 59)

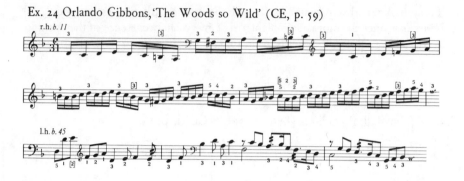

The bracketed fingerings are not in the original, but would have been under-stood by contemporary players. In b.13, group 2, the 2nd finger is placed on the wrong note in the original: it should be on the A, not the B. Mistakes of this kind are easy to make and need cause no surprise.

Ex. 25 Jan Pieterszoon Sweelinck, 'Echo Fantasia' (CE I/1, p. 86)

The fingerings are taken from an early-17th century MS copy (Berlin, Deutsche Staatsbib. MS Lynar A 1), which also gives fingering for five of Sweelinck's Toccatas: CE I/1, Nos. 15, 18, 19, 21, & 22. The 'good' fingers are generally the 1st, 3rd, & 5th, but sometimes the 2nd & 4th, as can be seen in r.h. bb.112–13, l.h. bb.120–21, and the table in Ex. 1.

Ex. 26 Johann Sebastian Bach, Fughetta, BWV 870a (*BG* 36, p. 224)

The only surviving examples of Bach's fingering are the Praeludium and Fughetta, BWV 870a (an early version of *Das Wohltemperierte Clavier*, II, No. 1), and two pieces from the *Clavierbüchlein vor Wilhelm Friedemann Bach*, 1720—the eight-bar Applicatio, BWV 994, and the Præambulum, BWV 930 (see Ex. 33, p. 78). As these were instructional pieces their fingering is fairly conservative; but Bach's normal fingering must have been much more advanced for his second son, Carl Philipp Emanuel, wrote in his *Versuch über die wahre Art das Clavier zu spielen*, 1753: 'My deceased father told me that in his youth he used to hear great men who employed their thumbs only when large stretches made it necessary. Because he lived at a time when a gradual but striking change in musical taste was taking place, he was obliged to devise a far more comprehensive fingering and especially to enlarge the role of the thumb.' (W. J. Mitchell's translation.)

Ex. 27 François Couperin, 'L'Atalante,' *Pièces de clavecin* II, Ordre 12

All Couperin's fingerings come from his treatise *L'Art de toucher le clavecin*, 1716 (enlarged ed. 1717). Some belong to six of the eight Preludes written specially for the book, and some to passages quoted from his *Pièces de clavecin*, Book 1 (1712) and Book 2 (1716–17). In the above example bb.22–24 show that he was more concerned with achieving a comfortable hand position (the long 3rd finger on the C-sharp regardless of its rhythmic position), than with making a 'good' finger coincide with a 'good' note. He drew special attention to the possibility of shifting hand position by changing fingers silently on a note (see l.h. bb.25, 49, & 50); and to a 'new' way of fingering consecutive thirds:

Ex. 28 François Couperin, *L'Art de toucher le clavecin*, 1716/17

The two alternative fingerings for the scale in thirds will of course produce entirely different effects, for the 'old' way makes legato impossible, whereas Couperin's 'new' way tends to group the notes in pairs:

Ex. 29 Idem

These are two obvious instances of how early types of keyboard fingering influenced articulation; but others less immediately apparent are also significant.

For example, though it is possible (with care) to play an upward and downward scale completely legato with the fingering:

it is far easier and more natural to break the legato at each shift of the hand, thus,

Similarly, the scale,

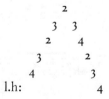

is much simpler when articulated,

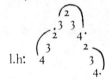

In short, the earliest types of fingering were ill-suited to long stretches of legato, and tended to sub-divide phrases into fairly small units.

The rhythmic effect of the articulation varied, however, for it depended not only on which finger was used as a pivot and which was crossed over, but also on which of the two was considered 'good'. Diruta, who regarded the 2nd & 4th fingers as 'good', would have fingered and articulated the following two scales in the ways shown:

Ex. 30 'Good' 2nd & 4th fingers (Diruta)

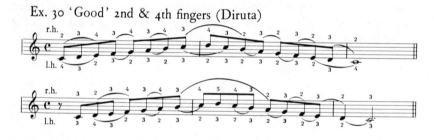

But the virginalists would have treated the scales differently, for they looked on the 1st, 3rd, & 5th fingers as 'good':

Ex. 31 'Good' 1st, 3rd & 5th fingers (Virginalists)

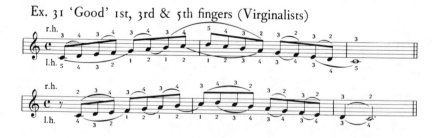

Ex. 30 shows that Diruta crossed 'bad' fingers over 'good' (except in l.h. descent), and that this resulted in articulation *against* the beat. The virginalists on the other hand, as can be seen from Ex. 31, crossed 'good' fingers over 'bad' (except in l.h. ascent), thus producing articulation *with* the beat. These inter-related facts can be summed up in the rule:

'Good' pivot fingers imply articulation *against* the beat.
'Bad'   „   „   „   „   *with*   „   „

Therefore, if we know which fingers a composer or school of composers regarded as 'good' (see Ex. 20), and are careful to associate them with 'good' notes, we can tell how any single-line conjunct diatonic passage is likely to have been articulated.

Fuller and more irregular textures cannot be dealt with so easily. In order to discover what effect fingering is likely to have had on their articulation, it will always be necessary to finger each passage in the appropriate style, using as model the known fingerings of the composer or school concerned, e.g. Exx. 20–9.

MODERN FINGERING

The basic principles of modern fingering first became widely known through C. P. E. Bach's *Versuch* of 1753, already mentioned. Originally it contained a supplement of six fully fingered sonatas (now available separately as C. P. E. Bach, *Sechs Sonaten*, ed. E. Doflein; Ed. Schott 2353/4 Mainz 1935), showing how the rules set out in the book's opening chapter were applied in practice.

Important features were: (a) the thumb used as pivot to achieve lateral movement of the hands; (b) thumb and 5th finger used on white notes only, except for wide stretches; (c) thumb passed under 2nd, 3rd, or 4th finger, but not under 5th; (d) thumb used for passages in thirds; (e) fingers changed silently on a note (see also Couperin, Ex. 27, p. 74); (f) an adjacent pair of black and white notes played legato by sliding one finger from the black note to the white.

Fingerings for all the major and minor scales were given, sometimes with two or three alternatives, e.g.:

Ex. 32 C. P. E. Bach's alternative fingerings for scale of G major

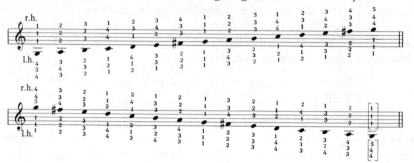

The fingering nearest the notes in either hand is the most usual, according to C. P. E. Bach, though a player of today would not always agree with him. Note that the long 3rd finger is still at times passed over the 4th in r.h. ascent and l.h. descent. As will be seen later, this is often useful when one hand has to play two contrapuntal parts. (See Choosing Fingering, p. 83.)

For broken-chord figuration he recommends the fingering that would be used for the chords in their unbroken form. This was already exemplified in his father's fingering of the Præambulum mentioned earlier:

Ex. 33 Johann Sebastian Bach, Præambulum, BWV 930, from
Clavierbüchlein vor Wilhelm Friedemann Bach, 1720

Though a detailed examination of the principles of modern fingering lies outside the scope of this book, some examples of fingering by composers, or their close associates, may be noted.

Domenico Scarlatti must have used a far more advanced type of fingering than most of his contemporaries, otherwise many of his Sonatas would have been unplayable. Though no autographs survive, the MS sources contain two interesting indications meaning, respectively, 'change the fingers' (probably 321321, etc), and 'with one finger' (i.e. glissando):

Ex. 34 Domenico Scarlatti
Sonata in D, K. 96 (L. 465)   Sonata in F, K. 379 (L. 73)

The preface to Jean-Philippe Rameau's *Pièces de clavecin*, 1724, includes a fully fingered 'Menuet en rondeau'. (Facsimile on p. 20 of CE, showing a misprint in b.13 where the r.h. A should be 2, not 3.) More indicative of Rameau's advanced style is the fingering he also gives in the preface for the unusual type of l.h. figuration found in his rondeau, 'Les Cyclopes':

Ex. 35 Jean-Philippe Rameau, 'Les Cyclopes' (CE p. 52)

In Haydn's Fantasie in C the r.h. demi-semiquaver octaves towards the end of the piece (bb.454, 456, & 458) were almost certainly intended as glissandos, for they could hardly have been played otherwise at the tempo indicated:

Ex. 36 Haydn, Fantasie in C, Hob. XVII/4

There can be no doubt whatever that octave glissandos in each hand were intended in the Prestissimo coda of the last movement of Beethoven's 'Waldstein' Sonata, for his pupil Czerny recorded the fact in Chapter 2 of his treatise, *Die Kunst des Vortrags*, 1842:

Ex. 37 Beethoven, Sonata in C, Op. 53, last movement

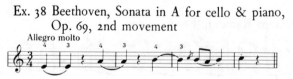

(Octave glissandos of this kind would have been quite practical on the early fortepiano, with its light and shallow touch. On a modern piano they are so difficult that it is wiser, whenever possible, to divide them (fingered) between the two hands.)

Czerny also clarified a puzzling passage in the 2nd movement of Beethoven's Cello Sonata in A, where pairs of identical r.h. notes are tied, but also fingered 43:

Ex. 38 Beethoven, Sonata in A for cello & piano,
Op. 69, 2nd movement

Here, he explained, the second (tied) note should be audibly repeated by the 3rd finger, with the first note played *molto tenuto* and the second unaccented staccato. The same effect is obviously intended by the tied (and fingered) pairs of r.h. notes in b.5 of the Adagio introduction to the last movement of the Sonata in A flat, Op. 110; and *possibly* by the tied pairs of r.h. chords in the 4th variation of the last movement of the Sonata in C minor, Op. 111—though this is less certain. The device appears to derive from the characteristic *Bebung* of the clavichord (see Chapter 1, p. 5, above).

Both Chopin and Liszt reverted at times to the practice of slipping the long 3rd finger over the 4th or 5th, particularly when the thumb was otherwise occupied and the 3rd finger could play a black note. Chopin's Étude in A minor, Op. 10/2, is based entirely on this device:

Ex. 39 Chopin, Étude in A minor, Op. 10/2

Though Brahms never included fingering in his piano works, other than arrangements and exercises, the music itself shows that he must have fingered wide-ranging arpeggios in an individual way. This consisted in dividing the arpeggio into complete handfuls, instead of part-handfuls, and relying on the pedal to mask the break in legato that occurred when jumping from the thumb to the 5th finger, or vice versa. The method will be clear from the following l.h. passage, to which normal fingering has been added above the stave and Brahmsian below:

Brahms, Capriccio in C, Op. 76/8

Here the normal fingering uses the thumb as a pivot to achieve a legato independent of the pedal; whereas the Brahmsian relies on the pedal to supply the legato between the 2nd and 3rd quavers of each bar.

In this particular passage there is little to choose between the two methods, since pedal must in any case be used. Elsewhere, Brahmsian fingering may be essential to the musical effect: e.g. in the following passage, where the downward crotchet-stems suggest not only that the arpeggio should be fingered in four-note handfuls, but also that a slight accent is required on the first note of each group:

Brahms, Rhapsody in E flat, Op. 119/4

CHOOSING FINGERING

One of the principal aims of good fingering is to avoid unnecessary hand movement. Hence it is often helpful to see how many notes of a phrase can be played legato without any hand-shift. If the whole phrase can be included, the player should then decide whether this fingering will best produce the articulation he requires, or whether it would be clearer with a less static hand position. For example, the following r.h. passage can be played without hand-shifts by using the fingering shown above the stave:

yet the articulation might be clearer and more precise if one of the lower fingerings were used instead, though all of these involve hand movement. In every instance the various alternatives should be weighed up, to see which will best produce the desired musical effect.

When shifts are necessary, they should if possible be made to underline the phrasing rather than contradict it; thus it is always an advantage if hand-shifts can be made to coincide with breaks in a phrase.

In passage-work the player should be continually on the look-out for patterns in the music—particularly the less obvious ones that begin off the beat—and should try to match them with fingering patterns. For example, the following left-hand passage from Bach's Fugue on a theme by Albinoni, BWV 951, (*S & I* II, p. 34) looks at first sight rather awkward:

but it is perfectly easy both to finger and to play as soon as it is realized that it consists of three phrases, as shown by the square brackets, each beginning on the second semiquaver of a four-note group, and each fingered 1243.

In passages founded on broken chords it is always helpful to reduce the chords to their unbroken form, as shown in Ex. 33, p. 78, as this indicates where the most natural hand-shifts occur.

In contrapuntal music and music that is mainly legato it is frequently necessary to revert to the old practice of crossing a long finger over a shorter one, thus:

the longer finger being used wherever possible on a black note.

A change of finger on a single note can be used for two precisely opposite effects: (a) to underline detached phrasing, as shown in the example on p. 82; and (b) to obtain a long legato. Couperin's example of a legato is given below, with his own fingering shown above the stave and the more usual modern fingering underneath:

When the detailed fingering of a passage has been worked out, its essential features should be written into the copy; but everything that is obvious or can be taken for granted should be omitted. Changes of hand position are important, and can generally be made clear for the right hand by marking the thumbs in ascending passages, and the third and fourth fingers in descending ones; and vice versa for the left hand. Any unexpected or irregular fingerings should also be marked, preferably only by means of the key finger involved. Otherwise the player's aim should be to reduce the fingering in his copy to the minimum consistent with clarity, for the fewer the marks the easier they are to read.

Further Reading

(See the following in Suggestions for Further Reading, pp. 177 ff.)

Bach, C. P. E., *Essay on the True Art of Playing Keyboard Instruments.*
Couperin, François, *L'Art de toucher le clavecin.*
Dolmetsch, Arnold, *The Interpretation of Music* . . .
Grove's Dictionary, under Fingering (keyboard).

6 Rhythmic Conventions

It is generally assumed nowadays that a composer writes the precise note-values and rhythms that he requires in performance; but this was not always so. During the pre-classical period, and in some cases as late as the 19th century, various notational and rhythmic conventions were recognized by both composer and performer, and to ignore them today is to falsify the music. Perhaps the most important of these conventions concerns the variable value of a dot following a note. In theory, if not always in practice, a dot is nowadays understood to increase the value of the preceding note by half. In the baroque period, however, the value of the dot, and the note on *either* side of it, depended on the musical context. Thus the group ♩. ♩ could mean anything from ♩ ♪ (as it does in some jazz today) to ♩.. ♬ (as in a military march); and Couperin could under-dot with impunity:

Ex. 40 François Couperin, 'Passacaille', *Pièces de clavecin* II, Ordre 8 (*EFKM* I, p. 56)

while Rameau could equally happily over-dot:

Ex. 41 Jean-Philippe Rameau, 'L'Enharmonique'
(CE p. 92, *S & I* I, p. 54)

This ambiguity arose partly because double-dotting was unknown before the mid-18th century; but the prime factor was musicians' lack of concern for precision of notation. A composer who wrote quickly, like Handel, might dash

down ♪ 𝅘𝅥𝅮𝅘𝅥𝅮.𝅘𝅥𝅮♩ , or ♪.𝅘𝅥𝅮𝅘𝅥𝅮♩ , or ♪ 𝅘𝅥𝅮𝅘𝅥𝅮♩ , or any combination of the

three, when in fact he required the perfectly regular though more awkwardly

written rhythm ♪· 𝅘𝅥𝅮𝅘𝅥𝅮.𝅘𝅥𝅮♩ . Even Bach, who was less haphazard in this respect,

sometimes used the same kind of shorthand. It seems certain, for example, that he intended the opening of his Partita No. 2 in C minor to sound like this:

Grave

𝄴 ♩ ♪ 𝅘𝅥𝅮𝅘𝅥𝅮♩ ♪ 𝅘𝅥𝅮𝅘𝅥𝅮│𝅘𝅥𝅮.𝅘𝅥𝅮𝅘𝅥𝅮𝅘𝅥𝅮𝅘𝅥𝅮♩ , although it is printed

Grave

𝄴 ♩ ♪ 𝅘𝅥𝅮𝅘𝅥𝅮♩ ♪ 𝅘𝅥𝅮𝅘𝅥𝅮│𝅘𝅥𝅮.𝅘𝅥𝅮𝅘𝅥𝅮𝅘𝅥𝅮𝅘𝅥𝅮♩ ; for his contemporary J. J. Quantz

wrote, 'If in a slow *Alla breve* or Common Time a semiquaver rest on an

accented beat is followed by dotted notes: ♪ 𝅘𝅥𝅮𝅘𝅥𝅮𝅘𝅥𝅮.𝅘𝅥𝅮𝅘𝅥𝅮𝅘𝅥𝅮 , you must play the

rest as though it were dotted and the following note as though it were a demi-semiquaver.' (*Versuch einer Anweisung die Flöte traversiere zu spielen*, 1752: English version, *On Playing the Flute*, trans. E. R. Reilly; Faber, London 1966, p. 226.)

Such notational quirks pose many problems, not all of which can be solved with certainty. Since hard and fast rules cannot be given, the player should look on the following notes merely as signposts to help him on his way; he will still encounter doubtful points, and these he must do his best to solve with the help of his own musical instinct and common sense.

VARIABLE DOTS

The value of a dot following a note in baroque music is variable: sometimes it has its present-day value, sometimes more and sometimes less. The following points should be noted:

(a) In contexts that are mainly rhythmic as opposed to melodic, dotted rhythms such as ♩♪ and ♩. ♪ tend to become double-dotted ♩..♪ or ♩. ♪, and ♩.. ♪ or ♩. ♪ in order to avoid a sluggish and heavy feeling. This is particularly so in slow, stately movements such as the opening section of a French Overture; but it is also true of any context in which the rhythmic aspect requires to be stressed.

(b) In the cadential formula ♩. ♪|♩ the player is often expected to shorten the quaver, and also to supply the missing trill, thus: ♩ ♩♪|♩ (see Chapter 8, Ornamentation, p. 112 below).

(c) The short note of a dotted pair should generally match the smallest prevailing note-value. Thus in a context of demi-semiquavers the written rhythm

♩♪♪♪♪♪♪ would be played ♩♪♪♪♪♪♪ , unless this conflicted with the

harmony.

(d) The written rhythm ♩. ♪♪♪ usually stands for ♩♪♪♪♪ , but can also mean ♩.♪♪♪♪ (see Shortened Upbeat Groups, p. 88). The important point to remember is that the dot is here (as always) a variable quantity, and it is up to the player to interpret it in the way that best suits the context.

This point is well illustrated by Bach's Fugue in D major from Book 2 of the '48', where the rhythm ♩♪♩ must be treated in two different ways if ungrammatical harmony is to be avoided. For in l.h. b.4 the 2nd beat must be played as written, otherwise it would produce consecutive octaves with the treble; whereas in b.22 the r.h. 3rd beat must be double-dotted in order to make harmonic sense with the bass. It will be found a useful exercise to go through the whole of this Fugue deciding which of the dotted groups should be played as written and which should be double-dotted. In doing so it will be necessary to decide between rival authorities concerning b.9, etc., where some say the r.h. should be double-dotted (e.g. Dolmetsch), while others hold that it should be played as written (e.g. Tovey). Possibly the latter alternative is preferable at this point, since it matches the prevailing semi-quavers in the r.h., and avoids the ugly progressions that would otherwise occur in the similar passage in bb. 18–19.

SHORTENED UPBEAT GROUPS

Allied to the shortening of a note following a dot is the shortening of what may be called an 'upbeat group', such as occurs frequently in French and French-influenced music. One example of this has already been given in para.

(d) of the preceding section, where it was pointed out that the figure ♩. ♬♬

might be interpreted as ♩. ♬♬ . But the shortening of upbeat note-

values can also be required when no dot is present. In an early autograph version of Bach's French Overture, BWV 831, most of the upbeat groups are written as semiquavers:

Ex. 42 Johann Sebastian Bach, Ouvertüre, BWV 831,
(Berlin, Deutsche Staatsbib. MS Bach P. 226, pp. 43–65)

But when Bach published the work in 1735 he made the notation more explicit, in case it should be misunderstood by the uninitiated amateur:

Ex. 43 Johann Sebastian Bach, Ouvertüre nach französischer Art,
BWV 831, from *Zweyter Teil der Clavier Übung*, 1735

Another interesting example of the convention can be found in Louis Couperin's Passacaille (No. 27 of the *Pièces de clavecin*, ed. Brunold-Dart), where the beginning of the *2ᵉ Couplet* is written thus:

Ex. 44a

though the sequential character of such an episode makes it almost certain that it should be played:

Ex. 44b

BINARY NOTATION FOR TERNARY

Perhaps the most puzzling of all rhythmic conventions is the use of written binary rhythms to stand for ternary rhythms. Primarily this means using binary notation (e.g. $\frac{3}{4}$) and ternary notation ($\frac{9}{8}$, or triplets in $\frac{3}{4}$) in a single piece, and relying on the performer to reduce the whole to ternary rhythm. Thus the Courante of Bach's French Suite No. 4 in E flat is written:

Ex. 45a

but would be played

Ex. 45b

It is hard to see any reason for this particular complication, yet the interpretation is undoubtedly correct since similar examples are given by Bach's son Carl Philipp Emanuel in his *Versuch über die wahre Art das Clavier zu spielen*, 1753, and by many other authorities. In the case of this Courante the solution is fairly straightforward; but unfortunately it is not always so, for further complications can arise; e.g. in the same context the rhythm ♩♩♪ might also be written ♩♩♩ ; while ♩♩♩ could appear as either ♩♩♩ or ♩♩♩ Such a chaotic state of affairs may be hard to credit; yet it can be demonstrated by one of Bach's own works, *The Art of Fugue*, where a single Fugue with a triplet theme happens to appear in four different guises, two rectus and two inversus, and at several points we find one and the same passage notated in two or even three entirely different ways:

Ex. 46 Johann Sebastian Bach, *Die Kunst der Fuge*, BWV 1080

From these examples it is clear that Bach did not make any attempt to be consistent in this type of notation: he was just as ready to use two different symbols to represent a single note-value, even within the same bar, as he was to represent two different note-values by a single symbol. This surprising fact should be remembered when studying an oddly notated movement like the following:

Ex. 47 Johann Sebastian Bach, Sonata No. 4 in C minor
for violin & keyboard, BWV 1017, 3rd movement

which should almost certainly be played thus:

It is also relevant to the Tempo di Gavotta from the Partita No. 6 in E minor, where the rhythm ¢ ♫♫ ♩♪ | ♩♪ ♩ in r.h. b.1 and elsewhere should probably be interpreted | ♫♫ ♩ ♪ | ♩ ♪♩ |, and ♩ ♫♫♫♫ ♩♪ | in l.h. b.6, etc. as | ♩ ♩.♫♫♫♫♫ ♩ ♪ | (see below, including Ex. 49, 12).

Stranger still, there are a number of Gigues written entirely in binary rhythm (e.g. C-time), though there is reason to believe that they should be played in ternary (e.g. $\frac{12}{8}$ or quick $\frac{3}{4}$). Two revealing examples are provided by Froberger. In his Suite VII of CE the Gigue appears in common time in the composer's autograph; yet in a manuscript copy made around 1660–70 (Paris, Bib. Nat., Rés. Vm⁷ 674/5, known as the 'Bauyn MS') the same Gigue appears in a different Suite (XXIII of CE), but now as a quick three-in-a-bar, thus:

Ex. 48

Similarly, the Gigue from Suite XIII appears in two versions: in C-time in the two separate editions published in Amsterdam about 1705 by the firms of Mortier and Roger, and in $\frac{12}{8}$ in a manuscript tablature of *c.* 1699 (Vienna,

Nationalbib., Codex 16798, f. 46).

The apparently perverse C-time notation becomes less inexplicable when it is remembered that binary-rhythm gigues stemmed from the 17th-century lutenists of France, who are likely to have played them with the characteristic French rubato known as *notes inégales*. According to this convention certain evenly written pairs of notes were played either long-short or short-long, with an effect that was closer to $^{12}_{8}$ or quick $^3_4$ than to C-time. (See *Notes inégales*, pp. 98 ff.) Such gigues, together presumably with their ternary-rhythm interpretation, spread to Germany and Austria, and were there adopted by keyboard composers, notably Froberger (who wrote thirteen), Böhm (who wrote two: in Suites Nos. 5 & 7 of CE), and Bach (who also wrote two: in the French Suite No. 1 in D minor and the Partita No. 6 in E minor). Though little documentary evidence for their interpretation exists[1], it is possible to compile a table of approximate rhythmic equivalents based on the two Froberger Gigues that occur in both binary and ternary rhythm. Values not found in these sources have been supplied by a process of elimination and deduction (see Ex. 49, pp. 94–5).

---

[1] The relevant references are quoted in Ray McIntyre's stimulating article 'On the interpretation of Bach's gigues', *The Musical Quarterly*, July 1965, vol. LI, No. 3, pp. 478–492.

Ex. 49 Suggested Ternary-rhythm

Binary-rhythm Gigue	Ternary interpre-tation

[1] Indicates an equivalent in Froberger's Suites VII & XXIII
[2] Indicates an equivalent in Froberger's Suite XIII

interpretation of Binary-rhythm Gigues

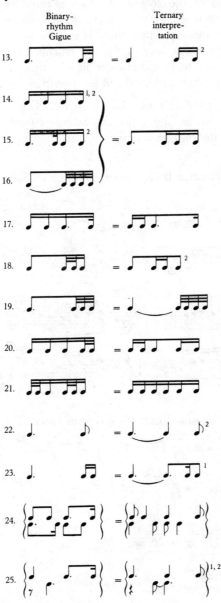

As will be apparent, the table in Ex. 49 leaves room for individual variation in details of interpretation; but this is scarcely surprising in a tradition depending entirely on extemporary application. If it is used, it will at least be found workable when applied to any of the movements concerned. Furthermore, it undoubtedly makes them sound more jig-like than any interpretation that slavishly reproduces their awkward and jerky written rhythms.

When applied to Bach's two binary-rhythm Gigues—by far the finest that exist—it results in the following interpretations, where A = Bach's notation and B = the suggested ternary form:

Ex. 50 Johann Sebastian Bach, Gigue from French Suite No. 1 in D minor

Ex. 51 Johann Sebastian Bach, Gigue from Partita No. 6 in E minor

Binary notation in place of ternary is found even in the 19th century. A striking example occurs in a Schubert slow movement which happens to exist in two versions: for the earlier gives the upper line of the r.h. part in binary rhythm (though carefully aligned in the autograph as shown below), while the later explicitly indicates ternary rhythm, which was obviously the interpretation originally intended:

Ex. 52 Schubert, 2nd movement of:-
Sonata in D flat, D. 567, ?1817   Sonata in E flat, D. 568, 1817

The slow movement of the Sonata in B flat, D.960, provides another example, for in r.h. b.52, beat 1, and elsewhere, the autograph *always* places the final demi-semiquaver directly above the last sextuplet semiquaver.

Chopin and Schumann also make use of the convention, sometimes in ways that are just as illogical as Bach's. Chopin here notates a single rhythmic effect in two different ways:

Ex. 53 Chopin, Nocturne in C minor, Op. 48/1, 1841

And Schumann goes still further by using three different notations for the one rhythm:

Ex. 54 Schumann, Romanze, Op. 32/3, 1838—39

Even Brahms reverts at times to the old convention, as in the following two-against-three passage which has true duple quavers in the right hand and spurious ones in the left:

Ex. 55 Brahms, Piano Concerto No. 2
in B flat, Op. 82 (1st movement) 1882

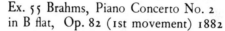

Since passages of this kind frequently occur side by side with those that are correctly notated (e.g. Exx. 53 & 55, above), it is always necessary to ask oneself whether a duple rhythm occurring in a triple-rhythm context is meant to be read literally, or whether it is an example of the convention that allows binary rhythm to represent ternary.

NOTES INÉGALES

The type of rhythmic freedom, or rubato, known as *notes inégales* is generally associated exclusively with French music of the 17th and 18th centuries; but though systematized most fully in France (see below) and used more consistently there than elsewhere, it was also recognized in other countries during the pre-classical period.

Briefly, *notes inégales* consist in altering the relative time-values of certain *pairs* of notes (never triplets), in order to intensify either their grace and charm or, on the contrary, their rhythmic vigour.

The practice was already known in 16th-century Spain, for the theorist Tomás de Sancta María wrote in 1565, when discussing good taste in playing, that in crotchet passages one should linger over the first note of every pair and hurry over the second, as though the first were a dotted-crotchet and the second a quaver:

Ex. 56 Tomás de Sancta María, *Arte de tañer fantasia*, 1565

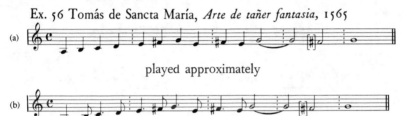

But he added significantly that this notation exaggerates the difference. And herein lies the essence of the matter, for the whole point of *notes inégales* is that their inequality should be so subtle that it cannot be notated in normal note-values. (The printed rhythms in the rest of this section are therefore only approximate.) Tomás also recommended three ways in which equal quavers could be varied:

Ex. 57 Tomás de Sancta María, *Idem*

As will be seen later, Exx. 56b & 57a give the lilting rhythm that the French called *lourer*, while 57b is the 'scotch snap' that was known as *couler*. The rubato shown in Ex. 57c remained unclassified.

There is no documentary proof that the greatest of all Spanish keyboard composers, Antonio de Cabezón, used *notes inégales*; but since he was a contemporary of Tomás and his works were published at much the same time as Tomás's treatise—i.e. in 1557 and posthumously in 1578—it seems likely that he would have done so.

By the beginning of the 17th century *notes inégales* were certainly in use in Italian vocal music, and to a certain extent at least in music for the keyboard. Giulio Caccini's collection of madrigals for a single voice includes the following among other examples of rubato:

Ex. 58 Giulio Caccini, *Nuove Musiche*, 1601/2

Here again we find the two French types already mentioned: *lourer* in (b), (c) and (d, 1st crotchet); and *couler* in (a) and (d, 2nd crotchet). In addition, (e) shows the 'shortened upbeat' discussed on pp. 88 f.

As regards keyboard music, Girolamo Frescobaldi wrote in the preface to his *Toccate e partite*, 1614:

> If you encounter a passage of quavers in one hand and semiquavers in the other . . . the hand that has the semiquavers must play them somewhat dotted—dotting not the first but the second, and so on.

This of course would produce the French *couler*,

A century later the Italian theorist, Pier Francesco Tosi, wrote in his treatise *Opinioni de' cantori antichi e moderni*, 1723 (trans. by J. E. Galliard as *Observations on the florid song*, 1742):

> The expression 'stealing the time' [i.e. tempo rubato] regards particularly the Vocal, or the Performance on a single Instrument, in the *Pathetick* and *Tender*; when the Bass goes an exactly regular Pace, the other part retards or anticipates in a singular manner, for the sake of expression.

Since neither Caccini nor Tosi, nor indeed Frescobaldi, gives very precise instructions as to exactly *where* these alterations should be used in Italian music, we may perhaps follow Tosi's hint by confining them to contexts that are 'pathetic and tender'. Since they are aspects of expression, they must ultimately depend for their use on what Frescobaldi called 'the good taste of the performer'.

From treatises such as Loulié's *Eléments*, 1696, Saint-Lambert's *Principes de clavecin*, 1702, etc., a fairly comprehensive set of 'rules' can be worked out for the use of *notes inégales* in French music of the second half of the 17th century and the whole of the 18th. It should be remembered, however, that early treatises are rarely as clear or as specific as could be wished, so it would be unwise to regard these rules as definitive. Nevertheless, it is certain that three kinds of *notes inégales* were recognized in France: (a) *lourer*, the most common, in which, for example, ♫ would become ♪ or ♫ ; (b) *couler*, in which ♫ becomes ♪. and (c) *pointer* or *piquer*, in which ♫ becomes ♫ or ♫ . And it is probable that they should be used under the following circumstances:

1. LOURER

When the time-signature is	pairs of notes in these time-values should generally be played long-short.
$\frac{3}{1}$	𝅗𝅥 𝅗𝅥
$\frac{3}{2}$	♩ ♩ and ♫
2, ¢ (as 2 in a bar), 3, $\frac{3}{4}, \frac{6}{4}, \frac{9}{4}, \frac{12}{4}$	♫
4, C , ¢ (as 4 in a bar), $\frac{4}{4}, \frac{2}{4}, \frac{3}{8}, \frac{4}{8}, \frac{6}{8}, \frac{9}{8}, \frac{12}{8}$	♬
$\frac{3}{16}, \frac{4}{16}, \frac{6}{16}, \frac{9}{16}, \frac{12}{16}$	♬

Exceptions: notes inégales are not used

(a) in passages of disjunct movement featuring harmony rather than melody;

(b) when a piece is headed *Notes égales, martelées, détachées, mouvement décidé* or *marqué*;

(c) when the notes are syncopated, or mixed up with rests;

(d) when they are merely repetitions of a single note;

(e) when they have dots, dashes or lines written above them, thus: 𝅘𝅥𝅘𝅥 , 𝅘𝅥𝅘𝅥 , or 𝅘𝅥𝅘𝅥 . (N.B. in French music of this period a staccato is implied by 𝅘𝅥 but *not* by 𝅘𝅥);

(f) when more than a single pair of notes are slurred together;

(g) when a pair of notes is marked 𝅘𝅥 or 𝅘𝅥 (see under *Couler* below);

(h) in very quick movements (here the first of every group of four notes may be lengthened, or all may be played evenly); and

(i) in vigorous or deliberately four-square movements where grace and charm would be out of keeping.

2. COULER

If a pair of notes is written with a slur and a dot 𝅘𝅥 , or sometimes 𝅘𝅥 , the rhythm should be altered to short-long 𝅘𝅥 .

3. POINTER OR PIQUER

If a pair of notes with the written rhythm 𝅘𝅥 appear in a context where an undotted pair 𝅘𝅥 would be played *louré*, the first pair should be played as though it were double-dotted 𝅘𝅥 . (See also Variable Dots, above.)

No hard and fast rules can be given for the degree of unevenness required by any of these *notes inégales*. Indeed, their whole point, as mentioned earlier, is that they should mean slightly different things at different times. The evidence of contemporary musical-boxes shows, however, that the unevenness ranged from $\frac{3}{4}$ plus $\frac{1}{4}$ (that is, exactly 𝅘𝅥) to $\frac{7}{12}$ plus $\frac{5}{12}$ (which is almost 𝅘𝅥);

and with this as a guide, the player must decide for himself exactly what is required by the character of the music in each instance. In doing so, he will not only be refining his rhythmic perception and musicianship, but also cultivating that *bon goût* which the French masters deemed so essential to the proper performance of their music.

Though no contemporary English writer refers to *notes inégales*, there is reason to believe that they came into use in England not long after the Restoration of the Monarchy in 1660. The devotion of Charles II to everything French prompted him to send the young Pelham Humfrey of the Chapel Royal to study in Paris, so that he might acquire the latest fashionable musical practices. On his return, Humfrey could hardly fail to reproduce these for the King's pleasure. Nor can the visit to England of Froberger in 1662 have been without its effect on his fellow musicians, for he too was strongly influenced by the French School. More important still is the evidence of rhythmic discrepancies in numerous variant sources of the music itself. These show, for example, that the prevailing rhythm of a single Alman might be notated as either ♩♩♩♩ or ♩.♩♩.♩ ; or, in a Corant, that one and the same passage could appear as either ♩. ♪♩ or ♩. ♫♩. The inference being that in both cases the French *lourer* was required—approximately ♩♩♩♩ (3 3) and ♩♩♩♪ (3) respectively—and the writers were uncertain how best to convey this subtle nuance to the uninitiated English amateur.

The French *couler* also appears to have been used, particularly when a slur was written over a pair of equal notes: e.g. ♩♩ = ♩♩ , or ♩♩ (3) . And, as usual, the variable value of the dot allowed ♩.♩ to represent anything from ♩♪ (3) to ♩..♩ or ♩ᵧ♩ .

Though it would be premature to attempt to codify the application of *notes inégales* to English music, there seems little doubt that they were in use at the time of Purcell; and that their effect was to shift flowing duple-time music towards triplet rhythm, and majestic or vigorous music towards double-dotting.

In Germany *notes inégales* of the *lourer* type are referred to in passing by Georg Muffat in the preface to his *Florilegium I*, 1695, much more fully by Quantz in his *Versuch* of 1752, and again fleetingly by C. P. E. Bach in his

Versuch of 1753. According to Quantz (Chap. XI, section 12: English version p. 123), pairs of the quickest notes in any moderate or slow tempo should be played long-short, with the exception of those listed under *Lourer* (d, g, & h), above. He also speaks of the shortening of a note or notes following a dot, but does not mention the *couler*. Yet the latter, curiously enough, was used by J. S. Bach at two points in the slow movement of his Harpsichord Concerto in D, BWV 1054, to replace the even semiquavers found in the original version of the work, the Violin Concerto in E, BWV 1042:

Ex. 59 Johann Sebastian Bach, Concerto, BWV 1042 & 1054, 2nd movement
BWV 1042, (Violin version)

BWV 1054, (Harpsichord version)

To sum up: it is hard to assess how much or how little *notes inégales* were used in countries other than France (where for a time they were obligatory) and England (where they appear to have been fashionable); but perhaps it would be fair to assume that they were generally regarded as an elegant embellishment to be employed occasionally rather than consistently, and more particularly in works written in, or strongly influenced by, the French style.

Further Reading

(See the following in Suggestions for Further Reading, pp. 177 ff.)

Borrel, Eugène, *L'Interprétation de la musique française.*
Couperin, François, *L'Art de toucher le clavecin.*
Dolmetsch, Arnold, *The Interpretation of Music . . .*
Donington, Robert, *The Interpretation of Early Music.*
Geoffroy-Dechaume, Antoine, *Les 'Secrets' de la musique ancienne.*
Grove's Dictionary, under Dotted Notes, Inégales.
Mellers, Wilfred H., *François Couperin . . .*
Quantz, J. J., *On Playing the Flute.*

7 The 'Tones' or Modes

Before the familiar system of major and minor tonality had been established, instrumental music was apparently based on a series of 'Tones' or Modes evolved from the earlier Church Modes.

The Church Modes were a codification, probably made during the 8th century, of the tonal aspect of Gregorian plainsong. They can be most easily described as 'white note' scales beginning on various degrees of the present-day scale of C major, and thus differing from one another in the order of their tone and semitone intervals. Originally there were eight: the four so-called Authentic Modes known as the Dorian, Phrygian, Lydian, and Mixolydian, which started on D, E, F, and G respectively; together with the Plagal counterpart of each, the Hypodorian, Hypophrygian, Hypolydian, and Hypomixolydian, starting a fourth lower than its companion but sharing the same 'final' or concluding note. (Ex. 60, Nos. 1–8.) In the mid-16th century the Swiss theorist Henricus Glareanus described two further pairs of modes in his treatise *Dodekachordon*, 1547, bringing the total to twelve. These were the Aeolian and Ionian, beginning on A and C respectively, plus their Plagal counterparts. (Ex. 60, Nos. 9–12.) (It will be noted that the Ionian Mode is the same as the modern scale of C major, and the Aeolian the same as the descending melodic form of A minor.)

Different classifications of the modes were proposed at various times, such as Charles Guillet's switching around of their names and numbers in his keyboard pieces, *24 Fantaisies à quatre parties disposées suivant les douze modes*, 1610. Although Guillet's classification was adopted by the lutenist Denis Gaultier, it was Glareanus's that provided the foundation for further significant developments.

During the second half of the 16th century the modes, as applied to instrumental music, were modified in various ways and became known as the 'Tones'. These still numbered either eight or twelve, as can be seen, for example, from the keyboard publications of Antonio de Cabezón (1578) and Andrea and

Ex. 60 Church Modes

after Henricus Glareanus,
Dodekachordon, 1547

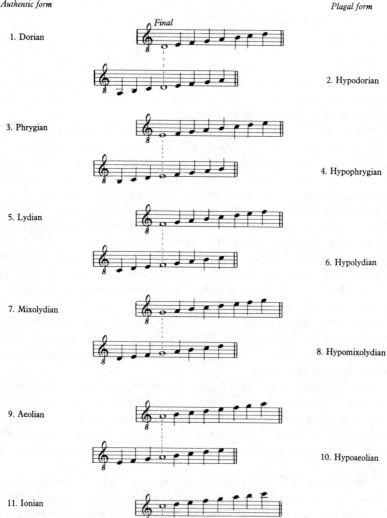

Authentic form

Plagal form

1. Dorian

Final

2. Hypodorian

3. Phrygian

4. Hypophrygian

5. Lydian

6. Hypolydian

7. Mixolydian

8. Hypomixolydian

9. Aeolian

10. Hypoaeolian

11. Ionian

12. Hypoionian

Ex. 61 Instrumental 'Tones'

after Cabezón (1578)
and A. & G. Gabrieli (1593)

after Bull MS (c. 1621)
Vienna, Nationalbib. MS 17771, f 221ᵛ

Giovanni Gabrieli (1593); but they were no longer grouped strictly in Authentic and Plagal pairs. Moreover, Tones 2, 6, & 11 now had a signature of one flat, and in each tone certain accidentals were permitted, though virtually none besides B flat and E flat, B natural, and F sharp, C sharp, and G sharp. Final cadences were prescribed; and intermediate cadences and modulations were restricted by the accidentals available, thus giving every Tone its individual flavour. The Tones might be transposed upwards a fourth or a fifth (or downwards a fifth or a fourth), but are shown in Ex. 61, left hand column, at their original pitch. Permitted accidentals are indicated above the stave, the less usual within brackets.

A drift towards major and minor tonality is already apparent, and becomes more marked with the onset of the 17th century. In a small manuscript book of pieces by John Bull dating from about 1621 (Vienna, Nationalbib. MS 17771), a table records the eight Tones recognized by the writer. They derive directly from Tones 1–8 of Cabezón and the Gabrielis, but their major and minor tendencies are still more obvious. (Ex. 61, right hand column.) This classification was in widespread use, and remained current in France (particularly for organ music) until at least the publication of Guilan's *Pièces d'orgue*, 1706.

The recognition of major and minor tonality was nevertheless virtually complete by the beginning of the 18th century. For the use of church modes in Georg Philipp Telemann's *XX kleine Fugen*, 1731, was a backward-looking attempt to reconcile the old style with the new. Each of these little pieces is headed by a group of letters, generally four in number, of which the first indicates the mode used; the second, the opening note; the third, a key touched during the course of the piece; and the fourth, the 'final'. The top part is confined, usually quite strictly, to one or other of the twelve modes of Glareanus, with the exception of the 4th and 12th (Hypophrygian and Hypoionian).

During the 19th century modal harmony made an occasional reappearance, generally in the context of some kind of national music, such as the Mazurkas of Chopin. But Beethoven's use of the Lydian Mode in his 'Heiliger Dankgesang eines Genesenen an die Gottheit'—the third movement of the String Quartet in A minor, Op. 132—was a direct reference, for a particular purpose, to the already archaic modal style of an earlier epoch.

(N.B. The instrumental Tones must not be confused with Psalm Tones. The latter are short plainsong melodies, based on the first eight Church Modes, to which the Psalms are sung in the Roman liturgy. They also provided *cantus firmi* for the organ versets, or interludes, used in *alternatim* performance: i.e. when alternate verses of a text were taken by choir and organ. See Chapter 2, p. 18 above, under Plainsong Settings.)

8 Ornamentation

The amount of ornamentation noted in keyboard music varies enormously from country to country, from composer to composer, and from source to source. It should be remembered, however, that ornaments of one kind or another were part and parcel of most pre-classical music; and if a composer did not always trouble to write them in his score (particularly when it was not intended for the printer), this was not because he wanted none to be heard, but because he relied on the player to supply ornaments wherever they were necessary. The player of today must therefore do likewise if he wishes to preserve the style of the music.

Extempore ornaments are most likely to be required at unornamented cadences (e.g. ♩ ♪ ♩ should generally have a shake on the first note), on long-held notes, and in later appearances of a theme whose initial ornamentation has been omitted. If such passages sound 'empty' in performance, either rhythmically or melodically, it is a sign that some decoration should be added. This may follow the pattern set by a fully ornamented work by the same composer, or, failing that, by a contemporary work written in a similar style.

Ornaments should be practised slowly to begin with. If this is done consistently, and the rhythm defined clearly from the start, it will be found that they soon become an integral part of the music.

GERMANY: PRE-CLASSICAL

The earliest known ornament sign in keyboard music is found in German sources such as the *Buxheimer Orgelbuch* of *c.* 1460–70. It consists of a loop added below a note: ♩ or ♩. This was named a *Mordant* in Johannes Buchner's *Fundamentum* of *c.* 1520, and explained by Elias Nicolaus Ammerbach in his *Orgel oder Instrument Tabulatur*, 1571, in the following complementary ways:

In an ascending passage the *mordant* indicates an alternation between the written
note and the note below, i.e.

and in a descending passage, an alternation between the written note and the
note above.

Thus it can be seen that (a) the ornament begins on the main note; (b) it is
likely to last half the value of the written note; (c) its direction is determined
by the context; and (d) it is related to both the later mordent and the shake-
beginning-on-the-main-note .

Another type of embellishment in early use was known as *Diminutio*, or
Divisions. Here the player replaced the written note by an extempore group
of notes of lesser value. (The term must not be confused with *diminution* in a
canon or fugue; see Chapter 2: Musical Types and Forms, under Pre-Classical
1, p. 13.) A 15th-century German manuscript (formerly Hamburg, Staatsbib.
ND VI 3225, but destroyed during World War II) listed thirty-eight formulae
that could be used for spanning the interval between two consecutive notes.
Among them were the following:

Like added shakes, these and similar embellishments are in place when a passage would sound uncomfortably static, either rhythmically or melodically, if played exactly as written. They need not be confined to the top part alone.

From the 17th century the signs used for ornaments in Germany became fairly standardized. Bach compiled a list of thirteen for the benefit of his eldest son, Wilhelm Friedemann, in a manuscript volume dated 1720. Together with seven additional signs (Nos. 14–20, below) these may be taken as representing Northern and Central German practice until about the mid-18th century. Bach's list and explanations are as follows:

'Explication'
from J. S. Bach's 'Klavierbüchlein vor Wilhelm Friedemann Bach', 1720

'Explanation of various signs,
showing how to play certain ornaments neatly'

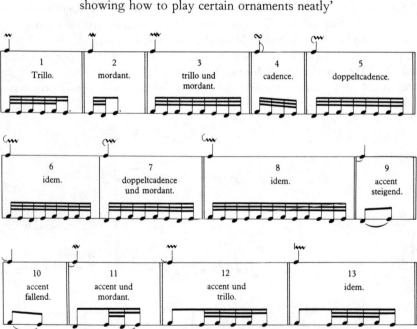

As a general rule these ornaments begin on the beat, and are played diatonically within the key that reigns at the moment. The number of repercussions depends on the context. The player should also remember the following points about individual ornaments (the numbers correspond to those in the table on the previous page):

1. The signs ∾, ∿, and *tr* are all used for the *trillo* or shake, and are equivalent to one another. (The first two are generally indistinguishable in contemporary MSS; while *tr* often turns into an indeterminate squiggle which can be easily confused with them, or with ∾ or ∿.) The shake begins on the note above, provided this does not produce ungrammatical harmony (consecutives, etc.), and its length depends on the context rather than on the particular sign used. (See also 20, *Schneller*, p. 117.) The *Explication* does not specify terminations for plain shakes 1 or their derivatives 5, 6, 12, & 13, but it is clear from both Johann Joachim Quantz (1752) and Carl Philipp Emanuel Bach (1753) that closing-notes are at times required even when they are not marked. Thus ♩♩ might be interpreted as either ♫♩.♩ or ♫♫♩ . Carl Philipp Emanuel says that closing-notes should be used at the end of a shake on a long note, and on a short note when the following note is one step higher (though not one step lower). But the ruling is so indefinite that the player must rely on his musical instinct as a guide: if the shape or flow of a phrase is improved by the addition of closing-notes, they should be used; if not, a plain shake is preferable. Often, of course, the closing-notes are included in the text, in a figure such as ♩.♫♩ where the two short notes become part of the ornament, i.e. ♩♫♩ ; and if the shake occurs as part of a dotted figure such as ♩.♫♩ , it should stop on the beat, thus ♩♫♩ or ♩♫♩ . When a shake is tied over to part of the following beat ♩♫♩ , it should stop short ♩♫♩ in order to indicate the tie. A slur from the preceding note ♩♩.♫♩ or ♩♩.♫♩ shows that the first auxiliary is tied ♩♫♩ .

2. The *mordant* or mordent ∿ is not necessarily restricted to three notes. In some contexts it is more effective to increase the number of repercussions to ♪♪♪♪ or ♪♪♪♪♪♪ . The signs ∿ and ∿ are sometimes used for a long mordent, and should not be confused with the shake-and-mordent sign ∿ .

4. The sign for a *cadence* or turn ∾ can be written horizontally, diagonally, or vertically. All three mean the same thing. When the sign occurs *between* two notes, the turn should be played after the main note has been struck, and spaced out as best fits the context; e.g. ♩ ♪♩ might be interpreted as ♪♪♪♪♪♩ or ♪♪♪♩ or ♪♪♪♪♩ .

7. This ornament would generally have more central repercussions than are shown in the realisation, like 8 or even longer.

9-12. In the *accent* or appoggiatura the small hook, or *Häkchen*, ⌣ is sometimes shown as a double-hook ◡ , and very frequently as a small note ♪♩ , ♪♩ , or ♩♩ . All mean the same thing.

J. S. Bach used several ornaments that are not shown in his *Explication*. The more important of these are listed below:

Ornaments used by J. S. Bach, but not included in his 'Explication'

14. The *Nachschlag* or 'after-beat' is one of the few Bach ornaments that anticipates the beat. If a passage in descending thirds is interspersed with appoggiatura-signs (⌣ or ◡ or small notes), thus : [musical notation] , the 'appoggiaturas' are played as *Nachschläge*, before the beat: [musical notation] .

15. Another, though rarer, ornament that anticipates the beat is the group of small notes, such as those found in the ornamented version of the three-part Sinfonia in E flat, BWV 791: [musical notation] .

16. The *Schleifer* or slide ♩ is interpreted thus [musical notation] .

17. *Arpeggio:* the sign ⎰ means that a chord should be broken (upwards, downwards, or both); while the word *arpeggio* or *arpegg.* added to a chordal

passage indicates that the chords should be broken, generally both upwards and downwards, as shown in Bach's Chromatic Fantasia, BWV 903, by the notation of the first half of b.28:

Each note would be held down after being struck (not merely the top one, as shown in the example) for the duration of the written value of the chord; and in such a context, crotchet chords would be broken in one direction only, while semibreve chords would be played up-and-down twice. Eight-note

chords might be spaced out ♩♩♩ , and nine-note chords

as continuous demi-semiquavers.

18. An appoggiatura in conjunction with an arpeggio should

be played thus: . (But see p. 127.)

19. Diagonal strokes written between the notes of a chord mean

that the chord should be broken and passing notes substituted for the strokes

thus: .

20. The *Schneller* (inverted mordent or upper mordent) is described by C. P. E. Bach (1753) and F. W. Marpurg (1755–56) thus: = .

Though not mentioned in J. S. Bach's *Explication*, it is likely that this interpretation (beginning on the main note rather than the auxiliary) was occasionally used for the sign ⌣ ; e.g. to avoid consecutives, or when there was insufficient time to play even a short shake. Nevertheless, the player should beware of making a habit of using this interpretation, since the shake beginning on the note above is much more idiomatic.

Handel's ornamentation is simpler than Bach's. In the Suites for keyboard he uses some half dozen of the ornaments given above: i.e. 1, 2, 4, 9, 10, 15 & 19, plus the sign *tr˜˜˜* standing for Bach's 3, *trillo und mordant*. In some slow movements we also find an unusual combination of small and normal-sized notes, e.g. in the opening Adagio of Suite II in F and the Air of Suite III in D minor, where the large notes outline the basic melody and the small notes provide embellishments typical of the Italian style. These movements show how an accomplished player of the period would add extempore ornaments to a plain melodic line.

Two outstanding treatises of the mid-18th century are Carl Philipp Emanuel Bach's *Versuch über die wahre Art das Clavier ʒu spielen*, 1752/1763 (English translation by William J. Mitchell, *Essay on the True Art of Playing Keyboard Instruments*; Cassell, London 1949), and Johann Joachim Quantz's *Versuch einer Anweisung die Flöte traversiere ʒu spielen*, 1752 (English translation by Edward J. Reilly, *On Playing the Flute*; Faber, London 1966), the latter being of much wider interest than its title would suggest.

The Southern German tradition of ornamentation was somewhat different from that of the North, for it was influenced initially by Italian practice (see under Italy, pp. 130 ff.). Johann Jakob Froberger copied his master Frescobaldi by using few ornament signs other than *tr*, *t*, and *˜* , all indicating shakes. Though he left no explanatory ornament table, it seems likely that these should begin on the main note, except in works written in the French style (i.e. the suites) where they would begin with the auxiliary. A curious feature of Froberger's notation is the comparative rarity of ties. Presumably he felt it was wiser to leave the player to decide when and where they were required, according to the sustaining power of the instrument in use at the time. This may have been one of the things alluded to by his pupil and patron, Sibylla, Dowager Duchess of Württemberg, when she wrote that his works could only be interpreted correctly by those who had either studied with him or heard him play. The precise implication of the direction *avec discrétion* (freely), of which he was so fond, would have been another such point of interpretation.

Georg Muffat in his *Apparatus musico-organisticus*, 1690, uses five signs of which four are not included in the list on pp. 114–17. They are: *t* = ordinary shake; *ł* = mordent; *ℓ* = shake with termination; *ℓ˜˜˜* = shake lasting the full length of the note; and — before a note = appoggiatura.

GERMANY: CLASSICAL

Fewer different ornament signs appear in classical music, yet even these are not always easy to interpret. In the main, classical ornamentation stemmed from the practice of C. P. E. Bach, though Mozart and (to a lesser extent) Haydn were influenced by the South German tradition, as exemplified in Leopold Mozart's *Versuch einer gründliche Violinschule*, 1756 (*Treatise on the Fundamental Principles of Violin Playing*). Around the turn of the century current theory was summed up in Daniel Gottlob Türk's *Klavierschule*, 1788, and Muzio Clementi's *Art of playing the pianoforte*, 1801. But the second half of the century was a time of transition, so certain features of contemporary practice can only be deduced from the works of the composers themselves.

The ornaments most frequently encountered are listed below together with hints concerning their interpretation.

1. *Triller* or shake: *tr*, ᴧᴧ, ᴧᴧᴧ.

In 18th-century music shakes both long and short begin on the beat and generally start with the upper auxiliary, at least in theory. In practice there are exceptions to the rule concerning the starting note, which will be discussed later.

Shakes are often preceded by one or more small notes. These should be played on the beat and included as part of the ornament. If the main note and the small one immediately before it are the same, the shake proper will start, as one would expect, with the auxiliary; if the small note is the same as the auxiliary, the shake must start on the main note; for the contiguous notes of a shake and its prefix should always differ.

More often than in the 17th century the sign *tr* is reserved for long shakes and ᴧᴧ for short; but the distinction cannot be relied on, since *tr* is sometimes found on a note so short that the only possible interpretation is a single quick appoggiatura. The sign ᴧᴧ is, however, less likely to be used where a long shake is required. Long shakes (with or without closing-notes) usually last for the whole written value of the note; but at times those without closing-notes end earlier on the main note.

Closing-notes are themselves often written into the text, either as an integral part of the rhythmic scheme, or extra-rhythmically as small notes. Their absence, however, cannot be taken as proof that none should be played, for composers often relied on the player to add them where they were required. As C. P. E. Bach wrote, 'An average ear can always tell whether closing-notes should be used or not.'

In the following instances a shake tends to begin on the main note rather than on the auxiliary:

(a) when it is preceded by a note, small or normal-sized, one legato step above the main note;

(b) when it is preceded by a three-note slide, upward or downward, whose middle note is the same as the main note;

(c) when the main note ends a diatonic or chromatic scale;

(d) in a continuous chain of shakes;

(e) in this type of figure: = (in very quick tempi this would be played as);

(f) occasionally in order to preserve the melodic line.

(g) In Schubert shakes begin more often on the main note than on the auxiliary.

2. *Mordent* or beat: , .

(a) short = or (on the beat);

(b) long = or (on the beat).

Sign (a) is sometimes written when a long mordent is intended; so the number of repercussions should be decided by the context rather than the sign.

Leopold Mozart gives = as one of two other interpretations of the mordent; but Haydn is the only important composer who uses it (see 7, below).

3. *Doppelschlag* or turn: .

(a) on the note = or (on the beat)

(b) after the note { = or

= or }

or some rhythmic variation of these notes. The two signs and used together mean (c) = ; (d) = .

Beethoven sometimes used the turn inaccurately, as in the Sonata in C,

Op. 2/3, I, b.45, etc., where   and in the Sonata in

B flat, Op. 22, II, b.20, where   .

For the signs that Haydn used for (a), see 7, p. 122.

4. *Vorschlag* or appoggiatura: written as a small note, ♩, ♪, ♪, ♪, ♪, ♪, ♪.
(♪ and ♪ are the 17th- and 18th-century way of writing an isolated semiquaver
and demi-semiquaver, and have nothing to do with the modern *acciaccatura*.)

The appoggiatura is played on the beat: and subtracts its value (not necessarily the one shown) from that of the following normal-sized note.

There are two main types:
(a) the long, which takes the accent and is usually, but not invariably, half the
value of the main note (a third or two-thirds as long when the main note is
dotted);
(b) the short, which is unaccented and quick.

Unfortunately the two types are seldom differentiated graphically, so the
player must decide which one is intended in each instance. It will be helpful if
he remembers that one of the main functions of a long appoggiatura is to supply
an expressive accent; hence, if the main note is already accentuated in some way,
the appoggiatura will tend to be short. This is most likely to occur in the
following instances:
i. when the main note is more discordant than the small one;
ii. when the main note is staccato;
iii. when there is an upward leap from the small note to the main one;
iv. occasionally, but by no means invariably, when the melody ascends and
returns immediately afterwards;
v. when the main note is accentuated in some other way.

It should also be remembered, however, that these are somewhat rough
generalizations. No hard and fast rule for the length of appoggiaturas can be
given, and here as elsewhere the player must allow himself to be guided by
his ear and instinct.

5. Groups of small notes
Though it is equally impossible to give any hard and fast ruling for the placing

of groups of small notes, it is useful to remember that they are often semi-realizations of an old ornament. If, therefore, there is a resemblance between the outline of the small notes and the realization of one of the older ornament-signs, the small notes should probably be interpreted in the same way as the ornament. Hence:

(a)   (on the beat)

(b)   (on the beat)

(c)   (*not* on the beat)

(d)   (on the beat)

(e)   (on the beat)

(f)   but with only the top note held (on the beat).

If both (b), on the beat, and (c), off the beat, are possible interpretations of a three-note group, the version that sounds the more musical should be chosen.

Other small-note groups are likely to come before the beat, and subtract their value from the preceding note.

6. Arpeggio:
The sign shows that the chord should be broken upwards, generally beginning on the beat, either quickly or slowly as the context suggests.

(Haydn and Mozart indicated an arpeggio by an oblique line drawn through the chord, but the sign is not reproduced in modern editions.)

7. The Haydn Ornament: ∿ (or ∿).

Though the signs are rarely reproduced accurately in printed editions old or new, Haydn wrote , or , or , instead of the normal turn , to represent . . (The latter is described by Leopold Mozart as a mordent, so the interpretation probably represents a South German tradition.) Haydn's usage is interestingly proved by one of his pieces for musical clock;

for while the autograph is written ♫ the clock, which still survives, plays ♫ .

The first of the above signs plus an appoggiatura ♪ probably stands for ♫ .

GERMANY AND ELSEWHERE: ROMANTIC

During the 19th century the use of ornament signs continued to decrease. Apart from shakes, mordents, turns, and arpeggios (respectively Nos. 1, 2, 3, & 6 in the Classical list beginning on p. 119, above), it became more and more usual to write out ornaments in full, either in normal-sized notes as an integral part of the rhythmic scheme, in small notes extra-rhythmically, or in a mixture of the two. Since the meaning of the few signs used did not always remain unchanged, the differences and similarities between Classical and Romantic practice are discussed below, together with some of the problems involving the interpretation of small notes.

1. Shake: *tr*, ⚡.

(a) short ♪ = ♫. or ♫ (generally, but not invariably, on the beat);

(b) long ♪ = ♫ or ♫ (on the beat).

In contrast to 18th-century practice, shakes now begin with the main note instead of the upper auxiliary, as can be seen from the Pianoforte Schools of Johann Nepomuk Hummel (1828) and Carl Czerny (1839). John Field may be an exception in this respect, for he was a pupil of Clementi, who followed the 18th-century rule. Nevertheless, at least one of his shakes—in b. 29 of the Nocturne No. 11 in E flat—sounds wrong if begun on the upper auxiliary. Some of the rest seem to require a start on the main note, while others need the auxiliary; so the player should make his choice according to the context.

Sign (a) no longer implies more than a three-note shake, sometimes called an inverted- or upper-mordent. Occasionally, if it occurs on a very short note, it must even be reduced to a single short appoggiatura, ♪ . Note that when the ornament is part of a chord, it still must be played on the beat:

The *tr* sign can also occasionally mean the same as sign (a) if it appears on a very short note. But generally it implies a shake with a greater number of repercussions, beginning on the main note and on the beat, lasting as long as the written value of the note, and ending on the main note.

Long shakes are often preceded by one or more small notes. These are generally (but not invariably) played on the beat and included as part of the ornament. If the main note and the small one immediately before it are the same, as often happens in Chopin, the shake proper should start with the auxiliary; for the contiguous notes of a shake and its prefix should always differ.

Closing-notes must sometimes be added to shakes when unmarked, but as a rule they are only required when included in the text, either as small notes or as an integral part of the rhythmic scheme.

2. Mordent: .

Generally written out in full in 19th-century music, either as part of the rhythmic scheme in large notes, or else in small notes: .

3. Turn: ∾ .

(a) on the note

(b) after the note

(on the beat)

(off the beat)

or some rhythmic variation of these notes. Both (a) and (b) are often written out in full, in large or small notes. In the latter case the ornament is played in one of the ways suggested above.

4. Short Appoggiatura: ♪ , ♪ , ♪ , etc. (The small crossed quaver (♪) no longer represents an alternative way of writing a semiquaver, but is now a sign in its own right meaning a short appoggiatura.)

In 19th-century music long appoggiaturas are almost invariably written out in normal sized notes as part of the rhythmic scheme, while small notes (of whatever denomination) are reserved for short appoggiaturas. Contemporary books of instruction all agree that the short appoggiatura should be played *on* the beat; but the music itself suggests that there must be many exceptions to the rule, and that they are likely to increase in number as the century progresses. The explanation is probably two-fold. Firstly, there is always a time-lag between theory and practice. And secondly, as composers and performers moved away from the period in which the old ornament signs were in constant use, they tended to forget their correct interpretation, and to accept the graphic position of the substituted small-note ornaments as an accurate indication of their rhythmic position. So much so, that the normal 20th-century practice is to play all grace-notes before the beat, unless the composer directs otherwise, as Ravel did in *Le Tombeau de Couperin* (1917) when imitating an earlier style.

At times, 19th-century composers indicated anticipatory appoggiaturas by placing them before the barline. But unfortunately appoggiaturas are not restricted to first beats, nor are composers always consistent, even in their own works; so we are often left in doubt as to what was intended. It seems certain, however, that a single-note appoggiatura always anticipates the beat when it is identical with the following note, whether this be large or small. (See section 6, Arpeggio, p. 127.) And it is probable that anticipation is also intended with many bass appoggiaturas that are followed by a leap to a higher note or chord, as these are merely a kind of pedal indication.

By the mid-19th century it seems likely that appoggiaturas come before the beat as a rule rather than as an exception. This can be deduced from a passage such as the fortissimo version of the march theme in Liszt's Ballade No. 1 (1848):

Here the l.h. appoggiaturas must be played as anticipations, otherwise the three-note chords that follow lose all their power through failing to coincide with the beats of the r.h. Moreover, the single r.h. appoggiatura must also be intended as an anticipation; for had Liszt meant it to be different from the rest, he would have drawn attention to the fact by using some such notation as

The Brahms Ballade in D minor, Op. 10/1 (*S & I* IV, p. 48), provides further confirmation of this new practice. Admittedly it would be possible throughout the piece to play the grace-notes on the beat, with the l.h. following the pattern . But if that were done, it would be necessary to play the r.h. first beat of b.64 as ; and this seems improbable, since it introduces the interval of a ninth, which has never hitherto appeared in the theme.

5. Groups of small notes.
As was pointed out earlier (see Classical, 5, pp. 121 f.) it is not possible to give hard and fast rules for the rhythmic placing of groups of small notes. Nevertheless it is often helpful to remember that they may be realizations, or part-realizations, of an old ornament. If, therefore, there is a resemblance between the outline of the small-note group and the realization of one of the older ornament-signs, the small notes should probably be interpreted rhythmically in the same way.

Helpful as such comparisons may be at times, it should be remembered that they are less consistently valid for the 19th century than for the 18th. For it seems likely, as pointed out in section 4, that anticipated grace-notes become more common as the 19th century advances. Small-note groups containing more than four notes are always likely to come before the beat, subtracting their value from the previous note.

6. Arpeggio: | and (.
Both these signs show that the chord should be broken upwards, either quickly or slowly as the context suggests. In theory the arpeggio should begin on the beat, and it generally does so if it occurs in the r.h. alone. When in the l.h. alone it often comes before the beat, its top note coinciding with the beat itself. An arpeggio sign extending over both staves implies that the chord should be broken continuously from the lowest to the highest note. If each hand has a separate sign, the hands should generally begin simultaneously, or with one hand (generally the r.h.) starting slightly after the other, the main consideration being to avoid a thin tonal effect.

When grace-notes are combined with arpeggios, the grace-note (or notes) should be interpolated immediately before the note nearest to which it stands:

This ornament must not be confused with the long-appoggiatura-plus-arpeggio of the Baroque period, where .

Note the following unusual notation in Chopin's Nocturne in F sharp minor, Op. 48/2, and several other of his works, where the apparent slur is really a curved arpeggio sign:

Arpeggios written out in small notes follow the same rules, at least in theory. Chopin certainly intended r.h. small-note arpeggios to be played on the beat, for he drew the following dotted lines in a pupil's copy of the Nocturnes:

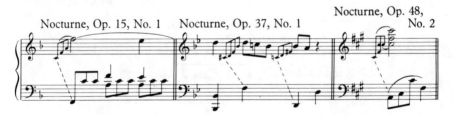

Nocturne, Op. 15, No. 1   Nocturne, Op. 37, No. 1   Nocturne, Op. 48, No. 2

In an ornament such as ⟨figure⟩ the first small D would also come on the beat. But if the first D were written separately, as in b.5 of the Nocturne in G minor: ⟨figure⟩ , the beat would coincide with the *second* small D; for, as we have seen in section 4, above, a single appoggiatura anticipates the beat when it is identical with the following note.

Other Romantic composers would appear to be less strict about starting small note arpeggios on the beat. In Mendelssohn's Song Without Words,

Op. 62/6 (the famous 'Spring Song'), the small-note broken chords almost certainly anticipate the beat throughout; likewise in his 'Venetian Gondola

Song', Op. 62/5: . In Schumann's Études

Symphoniques, Op. 13, the small-note downward arpeggios in the r.h. of

Etude IX also require anticipation,

otherwise the rhythmic bite of the descending scale of the theme is lost.

SPAIN: PRE-CLASSICAL

The Spanish treatise already mentioned, Tomás de Sancta María's *Arte de tañer fantasia*, 1565, describes two kinds of ornaments, the *Redoble* and the *Quiebro*, and provides examples of each:

Of the above, (b) is related to the early German *mordant*, whose direction is determined by the context (see Germany: Pre-Classical, p. 113); (c) is an extended shake beginning on the main note; (d) is a turn; and (a) is a combination of both types of (b), with or without a continuation.

Since no graphic signs are attached to these ornaments, their application was presumably left to the player; but Tomás does at least indicate that the simple *quiebro* (b) would be in place in the following instances (the added ornaments are shown in small type with downward stems):

i. In ascending or descending crotchet scale passages, on either the strong beat (a), or the weak beat (b), the latter being the more 'graceful'

ii. On two consecutive crotchets in a descending passage such as

iii. On a crotchet that follows a dotted minim in a descending passage

Tomás also describes and illustrates *Glosas*, or Divisions, the type of extempore embellishment that can be used to span the interval between two consecutive notes. (See under Germany: Pre-Classical, p. 113, above.) He adds that they are more likely to be required on semibreves and minims than on crotchets; that they need not be restricted to the top part; and that they should be added, whenever possible, to each appearance of a theme.

Antonio de Cabezón used no ornament signs; but his works, published in 1557 and posthumously in 1578, contain innumerable written-out decorations, most of them at cadences. A favourite formula was:

The second half of the penultimate bar is, in fact, a minim *glosa* on the note F sharp, or what Bach would have called a *trillo und mordant*:

Besides these written-out embellishments, Cabezón must have expected a player to add three-note *quiebros* wherever they might be required; for the preface to his posthumous volume, probably written by his son Hernando, states that a *quiebro* should be short, not long; as quick as possible; and played with either the 3rd & 4th or 2nd & 3rd fingers in the r.h., and the 3rd & 2nd or 2nd & 1st in the left. The fingerings specified might suggest that only the upper auxiliary was used. It seems more likely, however, that the figures indicate the fingers employed rather than their order, and that the direction of the auxiliary should depend, as in Tomás de Sancta María, on the context: i.e.

♫ in ascent and ♫ in descent.

ITALY: PRE-CLASSICAL

Fewer ornament-signs were used in Italy than in any country save Spain. Italian discussions on ornamentation are therefore mainly concerned with the improvisation of embellishments such as *Tremoli* and *Tremoletti* (shakes, long and short), *Accenti* (appoggiaturas), and *Groppi* (divisions).

Girolamo Diruta's treatise *Il transilvano*, 1593/1609, lists and discusses the following, which would doubtless have been used by Frescobaldi and other contemporaries:

Tremoli and tremoletti

Tremoli begin and end on the main note and last half its written length. *Tremoletti* are short *tremoli*. Both are diatonic, except where a cadence requires an accidental (see 11 & 12, below). They should be played lightly and nimbly, with the upper auxiliary, not the lower. (But see the 2nd group of 6, where the lower auxiliary is shown.) The ornament sometimes anticipates the beat, as in 5 and the last two groups of 6. (Diruta does not list the true baroque shake, which begins with the upper auxiliary and ends with a turn; but it can be found among his *groppi* in the last two groups of 11 and the last group of 12, below.) *Tremoli* may be introduced at the beginning of a Ricercar, a Canzon, or any other piece; also when either hand is playing a single line against two or more parts. The purpose of such ornaments, and of *accenti* (appoggiaturas), is to prolong the sound on a harpsichord or spinet, in imitation of the sustained tone of an organ.

Diruta gives some dozen examples of *groppi*, among which are the following:

These show that *groppi* may keep close to the original melodic outline (9 & 10), depart from it slightly (11), or treat it fairly freely (12); but the harmonic skeleton is always preserved.

As often happens in early treatises, Diruta's rules do not always agree with his examples. His most helpful advice may therefore be: 'If you want to play with taste and dexterity you should study the works of Signor Claudio [Merulo], where you will find everything needful.'

This can be seen from Ex. 62, which gives the beginning and end of Merulo's Canzon ditta La Leonora (for the complete piece see *EIKM* I, p. 38):

Ex. 62 Claudio Merulo, Canzon ditta La Leonora (*EIKM* I, p. 38)

In these few bars the following embellishments are used:

bar		normal sign		begins on
13.	2		=	the main note & *on* the beat
14.	1		=	the main note & *before* the beat
15.	2		=	the main note & *on* the beat
16.	38		=	the auxiliary & *on* the beat

Among his *groppi* are these:

17. bar 3

18. 4

19. 40

Longer and more varied decorations will be found elsewhere in the piece.

From Diruta's examples and Merulo's practice it can be seen that *groppi* are used to decorate conjunct lines and to fill in disjunct ones. At this period *tremoli*, or shakes, begin indifferently on the main note or the auxiliary, and may either coincide with the beat or anticipate it. In addition, we learn from Frescobaldi that the number of repercussions in a written-out shake is only shown schematically and may be increased at will.

Sometime during the mid-17th century the *tremolo* beginning on the main note and/or anticipating the beat was ousted by the true baroque shake, which begins with the auxiliary, coincides with the beat, and may or may not end with a turn. This can be seen from *The Art of Playing on the Violin*, London 1751, by Francesco Geminiani (1687–1762), where the list of ornaments includes the following:

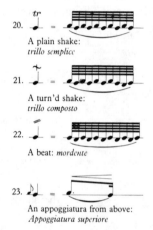

20. A plain shake: *trillo semplice*

21. A turn'd shake: *trillo composto*

22. A beat: *mordente*

23. An appoggiatura from above: *Appoggiatura superiore*

Diruta mentions *accenti* (appoggiaturas) but does not illustrate them. They were undoubtedly used from early times in both their long and short forms, and were sometimes written out fully as can be seen from one of Frescobaldi's 'Toccate per l'elevazione' in his *Fiori musicali*, 1635:

24.

These are of course short appoggiaturas, whereas the one shown in 23 is long.

Both coincide with the beat.

Domenico Scarlatti (1685–1757), true to the Italian tradition, used few ornament signs; and since he left no explanatory table, these must be interpreted in the light of contemporary practice. Unlike the French composers he used signs carelessly—or so the surviving MSS suggest; it would be a mistake therefore to aim at consistent interpretations. (The ornaments printed in Longo's complete edition are editorial realizations of those that appear in the MSS, and are often unreliable. Kenneth Gilbert's exemplary complete edition provides a faithful text.) A full study of the ornamentation can be found in Appendix IV of Ralph Kirkpatrick's *Domenico Scarlatti*: Princeton 1953. For present purposes it will be sufficient to remember the following points:

25. Small notes, ♩ ♪ ♪ ♪ and ♪ (as explained earlier, the last is the 18th-century way of writing an isolated semiquaver, and should not be confused with the later identical sign for an *acciaccatura*): all mean either long or short appoggiaturas on the beat. The length must be judged by the context, as the particular value used is not a reliable guide.

26. Groups of short notes should almost always be played *on* the beat; though just occasionally they must anticipate it, e.g. in a context such as

27. *tr* and ⌄ : both mean either a long or short shake beginning on the beat, and almost certainly starting with the upper auxiliary. Again the length must be judged by the context, as the two signs are used interchangeably. The player must also decide for himself whether or not a termination should be added, if none is included in normal-sized notes. (All the small-note terminations in Longo are editorial additions.)

28. Shakes following appoggiaturas. If the appoggiatura is above the main note: it implies either an ordinary shake or or a 'tied shake' ; if the appoggiatura is below: it implies either or . Once again the player must make his own choice.

29. The word *Tremulo* (entirely suppressed by Longo, but found in Kenneth Gilbert's edition) probably means that a shake should be made on the note or notes (generally the latter) to which it refers.

30. The meaning of a wavy line ----- following a note (also suppressed by Longo) is uncertain; but possibly it implies that the note should be held for longer than its written value.

As is usual in 18th-century music, ornaments are sometimes missing when consistency would lead one to expect them. In such places the player must decide whether this is a copyist's slip which should be remedied, or whether there is perhaps some reason for the omission.

One individual feature requiring special attention is Scarlatti's use of violent discords, generally as points of accent. Longo usually emasculates these by removing the discordant notes, as in the Sonata in D, L.206, where Scarlatti

in b.35, etc., writes [musical notation] and Longo substitutes

[musical notation] . The original discords sound magnificent on the

harpsichord, and certainly should not be suppressed on the piano; but the piano's thicker tone may at times make it advisable to thin out the sound somewhat by playing the chords as very quick arpeggios and releasing some of the notes. Thus the chords in the D major Sonata might be played:

[musical notation]

The sign ⸠ for an arpeggio does not appear in the Scarlatti MSS, and all those

in Longo are editorial; but arpeggiated chords, both quick and slow, are such an essential part of harpsichord technique that there is no doubt that Scarlatti used them continually.

FRANCE: PRE-CLASSICAL

In the majority of French keyboard sources the ornamentation is complete and notated with great care; hence no additional ornaments should be supplied by the performer, except in the comparatively rare cases of manuscript works that had not been prepared for the printer (see p. 144). This is true even of the earliest of the published sources, the seven small books of pieces for 'organ, spinet, clavichord and suchlike musical instruments' published by Pierre Attaingnant of Paris in 1530/31. Though these contain no ornament signs they include numerous written-out decorations, of which the commonest is:

(see *EFKM* I, p. 16). Like Cabezón's favourite ornament, this is the same as Bach's *trillo und mordant* ⌁ , i.e. a shake beginning on the auxiliary and ending with a turn (see Germany: Pre-Classical, 3, p. 114).

The first French harpsichord publication to use ornament signs and to provide an explanatory table was *Les pièces de clauessin*, 1670, by Jacques Champion de Chambonnières, the father of the French school. Most of his successors followed his example by including ornament tables with their printed works; but curiously enough these often differed from one another, not only in comprehensiveness but also, and most confusingly, in the signs used and the names given to them. The comparative table in Ex. 63 (see pp. 138–41) shows the usage of Chambonnières himself, of his pupil Jean-Henri d'Anglebert, and of François Couperin and Jean-Philippe Rameau, spanning in all the half-century 1670–1724. From this it can be seen that d'Anglebert's table provided the fullest information, and that Chambonnières's was somewhat shorter than either Couperin's or Rameau's. The most usual name for each ornament is given in the l.h. column.

F. Couperin, 1713

Rameau, 1724

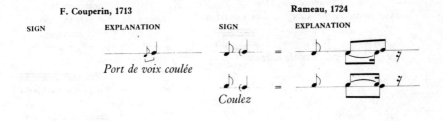

Port de voix coulée

Coulez

simple, double

Port de voix simple

Tremblement détaché

Cadence

Tremblement lié sans être appuyé

Cadence appuyée

Tremblement lié et appuyé

Cadence appuyée

Double cadence

Chambonnières, 1670

NAME OF ORNAMENT SIGN   EXPLANATION

d'Anglebert, 1687

SIGN   EXPLANATION

5. *Cadence*

Double cadence

(sans tremblement)

Cadence

Double cadence

*Double cadence
sur une tierce*

6. *Coulé*

or

*Coulé sur 2 notes
de suitte*

7. *Arpègement*

8. *Suspension*

9. *Aspiration*

Détaché

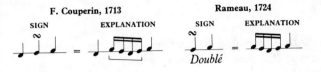

F. Couperin, 1713 Rameau, 1724

SIGN EXPLANATION SIGN EXPLANATION

Doublé

simple

figuré

Son coupé

The ornaments are played diatonically within the key that reigns at the moment, and generally begin on the beat (for exceptions, see 1, below). The following points concerning each should be noted.

1. *Port de voix* or appoggiatura. It is possible that Chambonnières's explanation is a misprint for ____, as given by his pupil d'Anglebert, for the repetition of a note within an ornament is unusual at this period.

Though Couperin does not indicate the length of a *port de voix*, d'Anglebert and Rameau give it half the value of the main note. In some contexts it may need to be either shorter or longer than this.

By way of exception to the normal rule, a *port de voix* anticipates the beat (a) when slurred to the preceding note, e.g.

(Couperin calls this an *accent*); and (b) when it joins two notes a third apart, e.g.

(more often than not this is in a descending passage, but d'Anglebert's *cheute sur 2 notes*, etc. also gives it in ascent).

In Louis Claude Daquin's *Ier livre de pièces de clavecin*, 1735, the following ornament is called a *port de voix* ; but it is in fact a combination of a *port de voix pincé* and a *suspension* (see respectively 3 & 8).

2. *Pincé* or mordent. Unlike the 19th-century mordent, this often contains more than three notes.

3. *Port de voix pincé*. It is odd that Couperin should have called this a *port de voix simple*. (Perhaps a misprint?) In the examples of d'Anglebert and Rameau the initial note has nothing to do with the ornament.

4. *Tremblement* or shake. Another terminological puzzle is Couperin's use of two names, *tremblement lié sans être appuyé* and *tremblement lié et appuyé*, for what appears to be the same ornament. (Rameau lists two different signs for this effect, as does Bach for the identical *accent und trillo* see Germany: Pre-Classical, 12 & 13, p. 114.)

In *L'Art de toucher le clavecin*, 1716/17, Couperin makes the following points concerning *tremblements*:

i. A shake of any considerable duration should begin more slowly than it ends.

ii. It has three components: (a) the *appui* or preparation, (b) the *battements*, and (c) the *point-d'arrêt*. The *appui* comes on the beat, and consists of a dwelling on the note above the main note; and the two remaining components follow. (Couperin's notation is ; but here he seems to be describing a *Tremblement appuyé* rather than a plain *Tremblement*. As with some other of his explanations, it looks as though he has mixed up his terms.)

iii. If a shake occurs on a short note the *point-d'arrêt*, or both *appui* and *point-d'arrêt*, may be omitted.

iv. Sometimes a shake should be played *aspiré*: that is, cut short by a rest.

5. *Cadence* or turn. Note that the same sign (∾) was used at different times for both the *cadence* (4-note turn beginning with the upper auxiliary) and the *double cadence* (5-note ornament beginning with the main note). D'Anglebert's second and third examples should have been called *cadences avec tremblement* (they are the same as Bach's *doppeltcadence*, see Germany: Pre-Classical, respectively 6 & 5, p. 114). His *double cadence sur une tierce* is most easily remembered as a turn on the lower note, starting after the upper note has been struck.

6. *Coulé* or slide. Do not confuse d'Anglebert's two-note signs (and) (meaning respectively an upward and a downward *coulé*) with his and Rameau's single-note signs (and) (meaning respectively a *port de voix* and a *pincé* though differently named).

7. *Arpègement* or arpeggio. It is easy to confuse Chambonnières's and Couperin's signs for upward and downward arpeggios, unless it is remembered that the hook in all four is printed near the note on which the arpeggio starts. In the signs used by d'Anglebert and Rameau the oblique line shows the direction of the arpeggio.

8. *Suspension*. For Daquin's combination of *port de voix pincé* and *suspension*, which he surprisingly calls a *port de voix*, see 1, above.

9. *Aspiration*. Couperin's and Rameau's dash (') implies an ordinary staccato, not a staccatissimo. In French harpsichord music a dot above or

below a note means something entirely different (see Chapter 6: Rhythmic Conventions, under *Notes inégales*, p. 102).

Returning for a moment to the subject of manuscript sources that were not prepared for the printer: the most important of these is the Bauyn MS (Paris, Bib.Nat. Vm⁷ 674/5), which includes more than eighty pieces omitted by Chambonnières from his *Les pièces de clauessin*, 1670, and almost all the works of Louis Couperin. Here and in similar cases—they are comparatively rare—additional ornamentation may be required; but never elsewhere in music by French keyboard composers.

ENGLAND: THE VIRGINALISTS

The problems of English keyboard ornamentation may best be considered under two headings: (a) the virginalists, and (b) post-Restoration composers.

In virginals music two principal ornament signs are found: (1) a single oblique stroke (sloping upwards towards the right) drawn either through the stem of a note, or above, below, or through a note without a stem:

1.

and (2) a pair of oblique strokes similarly placed:

2.

The second of the two signs is much the more common. Surprisingly enough, however, neither is explained or even mentioned by any contemporary authority, and both often occur inconsistently in different sources of the same piece.

A manuscript ornament table, late in date and of uncertain relevance, is ascribed to the composer Edward Bevin in British Library Add. MS 31403, of *c.* 1680–1700:

'Graces in play'
from British Library, Add. MS 31403, f. 5

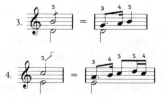

There is an exact parallel here between 3 and the virginalist single-stroke sign; but the three compound ornament-signs, 4, 5, & 6, are not found in any source whatever (not even in Bevin's own pieces from the same manuscript), though the single-stroke element of 4 & 5 and the double-stroke element of 5 & 6 are clearly similar to, respectively, the virginalist 1 & 2.

The earliest comprehensive ornament table in an English printed source appears in Christopher Simpson's *The Division-Violist*, 1659, which includes, among others, the following signs and explanations:

7. Beat

8. Backfall

9. Double Backfall

10. Elevation

11. Shaked beat

12. Backfall shaked

[1] 13. Double-Relish

---

[1] In John Playford's *A Brief Introduction to the Skill of Musicke*, 1667 and later editions, Simpson's ornament table is reproduced almost exactly. The one significant alteration is that Playford's sign for the *Double-relish* (13) is simply   which looks more logical.

Simpson's signs are not immediately relevant to the present discussion, but it is noteworthy that his realizations include all the elements of Bevin's ornaments: i.e. 3 = 10 (not in rhythm, but in shape); 4 = 10 & 8; 5 = 10 & the first group of 13; and 6 = the second group of 13. Striking, too, is the difference between the number of graces described by Simpson—he lists twelve in all—and the meagre couple of signs used by the virginalists. Yet Simpson's ornaments must reflect instrumental usage in the mid-17th century—probably earlier, indeed, for the codification of technique always lags behind its practice.

Such a discrepancy confirms what the music itself suggests: that there is no single consistently workable interpretation for either sign. This lack of precision, and the latitude it allows, would have been perfectly normal at a time when composers relied more on the performer's initiative than on details of notation.

How, then, are the signs to be interpreted in practice? It might be thought that variant sources would supply a clue, for sometimes a sign in one source is replaced by a written-out ornament in another. Unfortunately, however, the written-out versions are often as inconsistent as the placing of the signs themselves, so they provide no real answer.

A safer approach is to associate the more common double-stroke sign (2) with the commonest of all ornaments, which is a *shake*. Many are written out in full in the sources; but these are generally shakes with an ornamental ending or beginning. It seems not unlikely, therefore, that the double-stroke sign represents the even more important plain shake. If this is so, it still leaves the player a wide range of choice to suit different contexts, for the written-out shakes show that there are three basic types: (a) shakes with, and starting on, the note above (this is the most usual); (b) shakes with the note above, but starting on the main note (less usual, but by no means exceptional); and (c) shakes with the note below, starting on the main note (i.e. a mordent).

The inclusion of type (c) may be unexpected; yet this interpretation often provides the most satisfactory solution in practice, particularly if it is used in ascending passages, and type (b) in descending ones. Moreover, this alternative has a precedent in German keyboard music of the same period (see Germany: Pre-Classical, above, p. 113).

The length of the shake depends on the context. Occasionally it lasts the full value of the written note; but usually it is shorter, since it lacks the ornamental ending that would join it smoothly to its neighbour. In quick passages it may even be reduced to a single-note *acciaccatura*, either from above or below. Some of the possibilities are as follows:

As for the single-stroke sign (1): the one thing that seems reasonably certain is that it must represent something different from the double-stroke sign when the two occur in close juxtaposition. (Robert Donington, in his comprehensive article on 'Ornaments' in *Grove's Dictionary*, 5th ed., vol. VI, 1954, suggests that otherwise the single-stroke often 'does duty for the same ornaments as the double-stroke'.) If the two signs are to be differentiated, as seems reasonable, a hint may be taken both from Bevin (3) and from Simpson's more usual form of the same ornament (10). These would equate the single-stroke sign with the familiar *slide* or *slur*, an interpretation which sounds convincing in most contexts. When it does not, the allied *single appoggiatura from below* can be substituted. Hence:

Three further points concerning virginalist ornamentation should be noted:

1. The haphazard occurrence of ornaments in different sources of the same piece suggests that they were regarded merely as a pleasing embellishment to be added or omitted according to taste. For this reason the player need not feel bound to include all those that are shown. If he can play them fluently and effortlessly they will add a delightful sparkle and zest to the performance; but if not, he would be wise to thin them out considerably.

2. In written-out shakes the number of repercussions shown is only schematic. Either more *or fewer* may be required. Furthermore, when duple-time sextuplets are used the notes have only half their present-day value: i.e.

in a virginalist source is the equivalent of the present-day

♩♩♩♩♩♩♩ . Most editors modernize these values, but occasionally the
player must do so for himself.

3. It is sometimes necessary to add a shake to an unornamented cadence:

e.g. ♩ ♪♪ | ♩ may imply ♪♪♪♪♪♪ | ♩ , or some rhythmic variant
of this figure.

ENGLAND: POST-RESTORATION

The problems of post-Restoration ornamentation arise less from a lack of contemporary tables, than from the inaccuracy of those that have survived. Most of the mistakes they contain are easily corrected; but the evidence concerning one ornament, the *beat*, is so confused and contradictory that general agreement on its interpretation seems unlikely. The facts and their implications may be summarized as follows:

The earliest printed reference to keyboard ornaments is contained in Matthew Locke's *Melothesia*, 1673, which lists the names, but not the realizations, of the following five signs: forefall ⁄ ; backfall ⟍ ; shake ⁄ ; forefall & shake ⁄⁄ ; and beat ⌁ .

All the surviving tables which contain explanations, and cover the period concerned (i.e. up to *c.* 1720), can be shown to derive from a single source: that which provided the material for the four pages of anonymous 'Instructions for beginers' [sic] included in certain editions of Purcell's posthumous *A Choice Collection of Lessons for the Harpsichord or Spinnet*, 1696. The identical four pages of 'instructions' appear in the surviving early volumes of Walsh's serial publication, *The Harpsichord Master* (i.e. in *The Second Book*, 1700, and *The Third Book*, 1702); and are also found, but in a somewhat compressed three-page form, in Young's anthology, *A Choice Collection of Ayres*, 1700. The first book of the Walsh series, of which no copy is known, was announced in *The Post Boy*, 21–3 October 1697, as containing 'plain and easy instructions for Learners on the Spinnet or Harpsichord; written by the late famous Mr. H. Purcell, at the request of a particular Friend, and taken from his own Manuscript, never before publish'd, being the best extant . . .'; and this attribution is confirmed on the title-page of *The Third Book*. It would seem, therefore, that Purcell himself originally provided the material for the 'Instructions' included in all these volumes, though certain details suggest that he must have done so a considerable number of years before his death. Whether or not this is true, the ornament table included appears to have remained standard for the next twenty-five years or so. Unfortunately, however, it cannot have been an accurate reproduction of the original, for it contains certain oddities, as can be seen from the 'Rules for Graces' given in Purcell's *A Choice Collection of Lessons (1696)*:

'*Rules for Graces*'
from Purcell's 'A Choice Collection of Lessons'

16. Forefall

17. Backfall

18. Shake

19. Beat

20. Backfall and shake

21. Turn

22. Shake turned

23. Slur

24. Battery

It has always been obvious that the realization of the *battery* (24) was badly garbled, for it is patently a misreading of 34 (see p. 151), which would have been the normal notation for the period. Less obvious are two curious facts: firstly, there is no sign for a *mordent*, an ornament which was not only used widely throughout the continent, but was familiar in England, where it had been named the *beate* in Thomas Mace's instructional book for the lute, *Musick's Monument,* 1676; and secondly, there is no explanation of the compound ornament ⳩ , so often used by Purcell and his contemporaries.[1]

These several facts suggest that somewhere along the line—possibly in an intermediate copy of the original manuscript—the correct explanation of the *beat* (matching Mace's), and the name and sign for a *forefall & beat,* were both omitted by mistake; and that the realization of the *battery* was written so carelessly that it baffled the engraver(s). If this is so, the original table would have read as shown below, where square brackets indicate additions by the present editor:

Emended 'Rules for Graces'
from Purcell's 'A Choice Collection of Lessons'

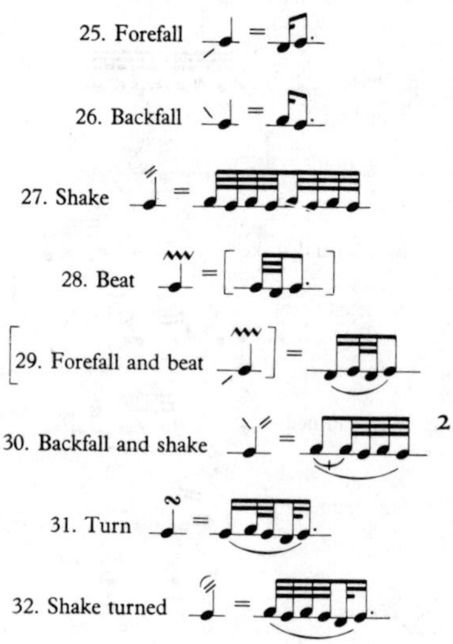

25. Forefall

26. Backfall

27. Shake

28. Beat

[29. Forefall and beat] =

30. Backfall and shake = [2]

31. Turn

32. Shake turned

[1] Christopher Simpson's *shaked beat* (see 11, above) appears at first sight to be related to 19, but in fact is not. His ornament is a *shake* on the *appoggiatura* (which he calls the *beat*), not a *mordent* on the main note.

[2] The editorial tie has been added to the realization of the *backfall & shake* on the analogy of the French *tremblement appuyé*.

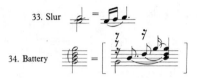

In a further explanation of the *backfall & shake*, the writer of the 'Rules for Graces' says that when the ornament occurs on an undotted note the *backfall* occupies half the value of the note and the *shake* the remaining half. If the note is dotted, the *backfall* lasts for the value of the note itself (that is, two-thirds of the whole), and the *shake* for the value of the dot (the remaining third). Practical experience suggests, however, that both *forefall* and *backfall* are apt to vary in length according to the context.

The foregoing summary (including the ornament table shown in 25–34) represents the present writer's interpretation of the facts as they apply to the period between roughly 1670 and 1725.

At a slightly later date—from *c.* 1725–30—the compound sign ⟋⌁ is used more and more rarely, suggesting that the *forefall* had at last become an integral part of the *beat*, and no longer required to be shown by a separate sign. In other words, a new generation had grown so accustomed to seeing the ornament wrongly described as ♪ = ♫♫ , that the definition was now accepted as correct. A slightly different realization, ♫♫ , was also current, as can be seen from various ornament tables and, most revealingly, in the fully written-out realizations printed in Nicolò Pasquali's *Art of Fingering the Harpsichord*, published in Edinburgh in 1760. Moreover, a number of signs other than ⌁ were now being used for the ornament, including ⌁⌁ , ⌁⌁ , ⌖ and ⟋. To add to the confusion, some of the same signs were used concurrently by other composers, such as Francesco Geminiani in *A Treatise of Good Taste in the Art of Musick*, 1749, and John Stanley in his *Ten Voluntaries, Op. 6*, 1752, to indicate a long and a short *mordent*, which they named indifferently both a *mordent* and a *beat*!

To conclude this somewhat involved survey of post-Restoration ornamentation, it is necessary to warn the student that the interpretation of the *beat* offered above is controversial, and would be judged by some authorities to be not only unacceptable, but also unnecessary. They would hold that the *mordent* proper

$$(\, = \, \text{ or } \,)$$

had no place in English keyboard music of this period; that the original realization of the *beat* (19) should be accepted at its face value; and that this is proved conclusively by a sentence in the 'Rules for Graces' which reads: 'Observe that you always *shake* from the note above, and *beat* from ye note or half note below, according to the key you play in'.

They may be right. But could not the word 'from' in this context imply 'to and from', rather than 'beginning with'? And is it really likely that English keyboard music at this particular period entirely ignored an ornament as universally familiar as the *mordent*?

Failing a decisive answer to these questions, the player must weigh up the evidence for himself, and decide which of the two views will in his opinion lead *consistently* to the most satisfactory interpretation of the music. If he agrees with the author, he will follow the realizations shown in the *Emended 'Rules for Graces'*; if not, the original version of the 'Rules' should be his guide.

Further Reading

(See the following in Suggestions for Further Reading, pp. 177 ff.)

Bach, C. P. E., *Essay on the True Art of Playing Keyboard Instruments.*
Badura-Skoda, Eva and Paul, *Interpreting Mozart on the Keyboard.*
Borrel, Eugène, *L'Interprétation de la musique française.*
Couperin, François, *L'Art de toucher le clavecin.*
Dannreuther, Edward, *Musical Ornamentation.*
Dolmetsch, Arnold, *The Interpretation of Music . . .*
Donington, Robert, *The Interpretation of Early Music.*
Dunn, John Petrie, *Ornamentation in the Works of Frederick Chopin.*
Emery, Walter, *Bach's Ornaments.*
Geoffroy-Dechaume, Antoine, *Les 'secrets' de la musique ancienne.*
Grove's Dictionary, under Ornamentation.
Kirkpatrick, Ralph, *Domenico Scarlatti.*
Mozart, J. G. Leopold, *A Treatise on the Fundamental Principles . . .*
Quantz, J. J., *On Playing the Flute.*
Schmitz, Hans-Peter, *Die Kunst der Verzierung im 18. Jahrhundert.*
Türk, Daniel Gottlob, *Klavierschule.*

9 Pianists' Problems

The present chapter is not concerned with questions of pianistic technique, but mainly with problems that arise when works written for earlier keyboard instruments are transferred to the modern piano.

Ideally, such music should be played on the instruments for which it was written. But since few of us possess a clavichord, a virginals, a harpsichord, and a fortepiano, we must often substitute the ubiquitous piano. And it is undoubtedly better to do that than not to play the music at all.

Happily there is little demand nowadays for 'pianistic' transcriptions or arrangements of early music. The pianist of today is expected to play what the composer wrote; but he must do so with a full understanding of the musical conventions that prevailed at the period concerned. In addition, he should beware of introducing anachronisms, such as pedal effects that were unobtainable on most of the earlier instruments; and avoid the temptation of trying to make his instrument sound like a completely different one. As the late Professor Thurston Dart wrote:

> Each instrument must be true to itself, and it must not try to ape the others. The harpsichordist must not fuss with the stops in order to try to make his instrument imitate the gradual increase and decrease of tone possible on the piano. The clavichordist must play delicately and expressively; a clavichord must never sound like a dwarf harpsichord. The pianist must resist the temptation to use octaves in imitation of the harpsichord's 16' and 4' stops, for the effect on his instrument can never be the same . . . The performances must also be stylish; they must be illuminated by the fullest possible knowledge of the special points of phrasing, ornamentation and tempo that were associated with the music when it was first heard. The performer has every right to decide for himself that some of these special points are best forgotten; but he must at least be aware that they once existed, and that they were at some time considered to be an essential feature of a pleasing performance. (*The Interpretation of Music*, p. 166–7.)

The main problems involved can best be discussed under four headings: Texture, Dynamics, Pedalling, and Limitations of Compass—though there is bound to be some overlapping between the first two.

TEXTURE

Contrapuntal textures form a large part of most music written before the mid-18th century. Though so easily reproduced on the transparently-toned clavichord, virginals, and harpsichord, they are far less suited to the modern piano with its rather 'thick' tone, over-rich in low harmonics. Special care must therefore be taken when using the piano for any kind of contrapuntal music.

The player's aim should be to achieve the lucid, 'stereoscopic' quality of sound typical of a string quartet or a well-trained group of madrigal singers. At first he will have to make a continuous effort to counteract the muscular habits formed by playing 19th-century piano music, whose characteristic texture consists of a top part of prime importance, a bass of secondary importance, and several subsidiary middle parts. This particular balance is such a pianistic commonplace that players tend to produce it automatically and unthinkingly, whether it is required by the music or not. Yet a moment's reflection will show that it is utterly foreign to contrapuntal music, where the individual parts are potentially of equal importance, though their inter-relationship is shifting continually.

In order to reproduce this type of texture convincingly a pianist must train his mind, ears, and fingers to follow the course of individual contrapuntal lines, as well as their combined effect, so that he may present the listener with a true picture of the ever-changing whole. He might perhaps think of the music as a kind of conversation, in which the interest shifts continually from person to person, and each one makes his contribution without unduly raising his voice. The chosen dynamic range should not be too great (a true fortissimo is rare, since several people shouting different things at the same time will never make themselves understood); and touch and tone should on the whole be lighter than in homophonic music. A semi-legato is more usual than a legatissimo, particularly if the notes are quick-moving, since it promotes clarity; furthermore, it allows freer play for the subtle kaleidoscopic changes of thought and mood that are particularly characteristic of Bach. The sustaining pedal must be used with great care if it is not to sound anachronistic: it should never be allowed to obscure the line, or produce the kind of impressionistic haze that is only suited to a later type of music. Indeed, haze of any kind is out of place, for all early music demands the clear line of an engraving rather than the atmosphere of an etching.

In specifically fugal music the student may find it helpful to remember the following points:

1. 'Characterize' all fugue subjects by means of carefully chosen articulation. (See Chapter 4: Phrasing and Articulation, p. 57.)

2. Make sure that the articulation chosen for the main subject is contrasted with that required by the countersubject, and by subjects 2 & 3 if the fugue happens to be double or triple. This will ensure that each remains distinct when several occur together.

3. Characterize the episodes of the fugue in the same sort of way.

4. Keep the texture as light as possible, particularly (when compared with homophonic music) the top and bottom lines.

5. Do not feel that the subject must always stand out as though it were played on a solo trumpet. The other parts are equally (and sometimes more) important.

6. If you *do* want to bring out a particular part, stress it only very slightly. Its characterization, coupled with the generally light texture, will do the rest.

7. A moving part will always stand out more clearly than a static one; hence, if an even balance is required, the part that moves most requires the least stress.

8. Always aim for clarity.

Even in Classical and early Romantic keyboard music the difference between the old and the modern type of instrument must be borne in mind.

If the sound of a fortepiano is compared with that of a pianoforte the first thing that strikes one is the smaller power of the older instrument. Less immediately noticeable, but far more important, is its different tonal quality. Throughout its compass the fortepiano has a tone that is bright, delicate, and somewhat thin, with an 'edge' or attack that is almost as sharply defined as that of a harpsichord. Indeed, it is possible at times to mistake a fortepiano for a harpsichord, whereas a pianoforte could never be mistaken for either.

When a player sets out to interpret fortepiano music on the pianoforte he should therefore remember that special care must be taken to avoid a thickness of sound that was quite foreign to the fortepiano, but is all too characteristic of the pianoforte. This is particularly important with close-position chords in the bass. These sound clear and transparent on an early instrument; but on the thicker-toned piano of today they must be played with great care if a muddy and opaque sound is to be avoided. The most obvious solution is to lighten the middle notes of the chord, so that they are less prominent than the octave played by the fifth finger and thumb. But at times it may be found better—particularly if a strong yet transparent accent is required—to break the chord slightly: i.e. play it as a very quick arpeggio. This practice was a commonplace of harpsichord playing, and is by no means out of place in piano music provided it does not degenerate into a thoughtless habit.

Differences of touch between the early and modern instruments pose fewer problems; but occasionally we come across passages that would have been comparatively easy with the light and shallow touch of the fortepiano, whereas they are extremely difficult, if not impossible, with the deeper and heavier key-action of today. The repeated triplet octaves in the r.h. part of Schubert's song 'Der Erlkönig', for example, were originally not particularly hard to play; but for the modern pianist they have become a virtuoso athletic feat. Similarly, the fairly rare rhythmic octave-glissandos, such as are found in the last movement of Beethoven's 'Waldstein' Sonata, Op. 53 (bb.465–474), and towards the end of Haydn's Fantasia in C, Hob. XVII, 4 (bb.454–458) (see p. 80, Exx. 36 & 37), would have been easy on an instrument with a light, shallow touch; but they are so hard to control on most modern pianos that it is safer, wherever possible, to re-arrange them between the two hands.

The tonal consequences of the gradual metamorphosis of the fortepiano into the pianoforte will be discussed towards the end of the following section.

DYNAMICS

Dynamic indications are rare in music written before the mid-18th century; but this does not mean that composers wished their works to be played at a uniform dynamic level. Dynamic inflection is inherent in vocal music, since it is difficult to avoid singing a high note louder than a low one; and it is also natural to all instruments other than those belonging to the organ and harpsichord families. Composers from the earliest times must have recognized this effect, even if they did not indicate it in their scores; and they would have expected performers, wherever possible, to make use of it. A pianist or clavichordist should certainly do so, for to restrict himself to the more limited dynamic possibilities of the harpsichord would be to deny an essential characteristic of his own instrument. How then should he set about the task of supplying the missing indications?

For present purposes dynamics can be divided into two types: (a) inflectional dynamics, which may best be compared to the rise and fall of a speaking voice; and (b) structural dynamics, which (to continue the analogy) mirror the contrast between a single voice and the combined voices of a crowd. The two types are not mutually exclusive: they overlap continually, and both are fundamental to music.

Among old keyboard instruments the clavichord is ideally fitted to reproduce inflectional dynamics; and though the harpsichord can only hint at these, it is perfectly adapted to the display of structural dynamics by reason of the clear-cut contrast between its two manuals. When performing old music on the piano, it is important to bear both these instrumental characteristics in mind.

To determine inflectional dynamics it will generally be found helpful to think of the music in terms of the voice. The melodic rise and fall tends to be echoed by a dynamic rise and fall; and though this must at times give way to other considerations, it usually provides a useful starting point. The phrasing is also an important factor: for the shape of a phrase conditions its dynamics, and dynamics help to define the phrase. Hence it is important for the player to decide where the climax of a phrase occurs—it may or may not coincide with the melodic peak—and what relationship it bears to neighbouring phrases. (See Chapter 4: Phrasing and Articulation, pp. 53 ff.) The harmony must also be considered. Discord implies tension and hence accent, while concord implies relaxation and lack of accent; thus a cadence, as its name suggests, generally requires a dynamic fall.

The keyboard layout used by an idiomatic harpsichord composer such as Scarlatti or Couperin often incorporates its own dynamics. The texture will be thinned out in order to tail-off a phrase; or, on the contrary, a thick chord will be introduced when an accent is needed. On the harpsichord these changes in texture automatically produce the effect required; but the pianist must learn to recognize them when he sees them on the printed page, so that in performance he may reproduce them clearly in terms of pianistic dynamics.

Generally speaking, inflectional dynamics in early music operate on a more restricted scale than in the works of Classical and Romantic composers. The sort of dramatic contrasts and changes that are natural to Beethoven would usually be out of place in Byrd, Couperin, or Bach—though a surprisingly wide range is covered by some of Bach's Toccatas and Fantasies, and similar works. But a subtle degree of dynamic fluctuation is always inherent in the music, and to ignore this is to reduce a performance to the level of typewriting.

The most important example of structural dynamics is the use of the two manuals of a harpsichord to reproduce the tutti and solo elements in Ritornello or Concerto form, which forms the basis of so many of Bach's large-scale instrumental and vocal works. (See Chapter 2: Musical Types and Forms, 4, Arrangements or imitations of songs, p. 19.) Bach himself indicated the necessary manual-changes in his Italian Concerto and French Overture, both for solo harpsichord, whose first movements are so fully marked that they can be used as patterns for every movement of this type. The words *forte* and *piano* here stand for the two contrasting manuals of the instrument. A *forte* in both hands represents a tutti; while a solo passage is shown either by a *forte* in one hand and a *piano* in the other, or by a *piano* in both. (An unmarked opening is understood, as usual, to be *forte*.)

When transferring this effect to the piano it must be remembered that the essential contrast is between tutti and solo, rather than between *forte* and *piano*. That is to say, the two-handed *forte* of a tutti passage must be differentiated from the single-handed *forte* of a solo; for on a harpsichord the latter, in combination with the *piano* of the remaining hand, would in fact produce the effect of a *mezzo-forte*. If this distinction is not made, the contrast between solo and tutti is obscured and the whole structure endangered. It should be remembered, too, that on the piano inflectional dynamics are required within the broader contrasts of solo and tutti.

Another use of structural dynamics is to underline the contrast between different sections of large-scale works such as Toccatas. The more brilliant and rhetorical sections would be played on the lower manual of a harpsichord and the more reflective ones on the upper; and this broad contrast should be made clear when such works are transferred to the piano.

The two manuals of a harpsichord can also be used purely for effects of colour. Thus the single *forte* and *piano* at the beginning of the slow movement of the Italian Concerto have no structural purpose, but merely show that the right hand is the solo and the left hand the accompaniment throughout. A pianist would produce this effect almost without thinking, for it is suggested by the very texture of the music.

Another common use of the two contrasting manuals is to obtain echo effects. These may be intended by the composer even when unmarked; but the pianist should beware of introducing them indiscriminately, whenever he happens to find a phrase that is exactly repeated, for they can chop up the music to such an extent that it sounds irritatingly short-winded.

From the mid-18th century onwards dynamic markings were used increasingly frequently. In works that had not been prepared for the engraver, however, they are sometimes incomplete or missing altogether. And even in works published during the composer's lifetime there are occasionally no dynamics whatever. In these various instances the player must supply what is missing, basing his additions, as with phrasing and articulation, on the known practice of the composer concerned. He should also bear in mind the fact that dynamics tend to become increasingly dramatic during the classical period, until they culminate in Beethoven's explosive and very individual style.

The extreme dynamic marks of *pp* and *ff* are unusual in the keyboard works of Haydn and Mozart, and correspondingly significant when they do occur. The basic marks are *p* and *f*; and the contrast between these two is still, as it was at an earlier period, of fundamental importance. Not that *p* and *f* should ever be regarded as having any absolute value, or as allowing no change within themselves. On the contrary, they stand for a greater variety of dynamic levels in early classical music than they do today, for *mf* was then comparatively rare, *pf* (*poco forte*) and *mezza voce* rarer still, and *mp* non-existent; and though the broad contrast between *f* and *p* must always be maintained, it is not only allowable but essential to use dynamic inflections within these levels. It may even be necessary at times, particularly in the earlier and less fully marked scores of the period, to bridge the gap between *piano* and *forte* by adding a crescendo or diminuendo. Haydn and Mozart used both indications in their fully marked scores (the Mozart Rondo in A minor, K.511, is a good instance); and for accents employed a variety of signs: *fp*, *mfp*, *sfp*, *sf*, and *fz*. All of the latter should be interpreted in relation to their context rather than as *fortes* pure and simple.

Beethoven's dynamic marks are more extreme than those of Haydn and Mozart, the whole range from *pp* to *ff* being normal rather than exceptional in his piano music. They are also fuller and more precise. As a rule it can be taken that any dynamic mark in Beethoven remains in force until it is contradicted; and that accents, including *sfs*, should be read within the prevailing dynamic level. But occasionally one encounters ambiguities and uncertainties. In the exposition of the first movement of the Sonata in D, Op. 10/3, for example, there is a *cresc.* in b.72 which is left without a defined termination. Should there be a *f* on the last beat of b.74? Or, as seems more likely, has Beethoven forgotten the *p* (*subito* implied) on the same beat, which would make the passage match the sequence four and eight bars later? Such puzzles can sometimes be solved by reference to parallel passages elsewhere in the movement. When this is not possible the player must rely on the promptings of his instinct.

The word *cresc.* is used idiosyncratically by Beethoven in two slightly different ways. Normally it means that the increase in volume should continue to the level of the next mark, as in *cresc.– – –f.* But when the next mark happens to be a *p*, it generally implies that the *p* should be read as *subito*, that is, as a drop from the level attained immediately before it. At times, too, it will be found that Beethoven uses the mark *sf* to indicate the peak of a crescendo.

Schubert's vocabulary of dynamics is very similar to Beethoven's, though far less meticulous. He had one peculiarity of handwriting, however, which should be borne in mind. His accent sign (>) was often so sprawlingly written that editors have mistaken it for, and printed it as, a hairpin diminuendo (⟍⟍⟍). If therefore the player comes across a printed hairpin diminuendo that does not seem to make sense, he should ask himself whether it was not perhaps intended by Schubert as an accent. Inconsistencies also occur from time to time. A *pp* may be followed by a long *dim.*, only to end up with another *pp*; or a *f cresc.* lead to no more than another *f.* In such cases the player must use his own judgement to decide at what level the passage begins and ends, and how the *dim.* or *cresc.* should be spaced out. Another odd marking is Schubert's compound sign *fp*⟍⟍⟍. It has been suggested that it means *f*⟍⟍⟍*p*, but this is by no means certain.

As pointed out earlier (see Chapter 1: The Instruments, under Fortepiano and Pianoforte), the piano for which 19th-century composers wrote was gradually changing in character. Instruments used by Mendelssohn, Chopin, and Schumann were closer to our own than to a fortepiano; nevertheless they were still considerably less 'thick' and powerful than a modern grand. Mendelssohn in particular must have preferred a touch and tone that was distinctly on the light side, for this would have suited the quick and delicate *pp* staccato effects of which he was so fond. He must also have been accustomed to a bass register that was transparent rather than powerful. If these facts are not borne in mind when playing Mendelssohn today, the heavier quality of our pianos will continually distort his typically light and delicate texture.

With Chopin and Schumann the situation is less straightforward. Their music at times seems to reach out towards the weight and power of the modern pianoforte; yet it should never be forgotten that both composers wrote essentially for an intimate group of listeners in a *salon* or drawing-room, rather than for a more impersonal audience in a large concert hall. Hence, sensitiveness was of greater importance to them than sheer dynamic power. Chopin was delighted when Kalkbrenner mistakenly guessed from his playing that he had been a pupil of Field; and he preferred, as we know, a piano whose touch was much lighter than that used by many performers of his day. A. J. Hipkins of the firm of Broadwood, whose pianos Chopin used in England, wrote that his fortissimo was a full, pure tone without any suspicion of harshness or noise; that his nuances decreased to the faintest yet always distinct pianissimo; and that his singing legatissimo touch was specially remarkable. Schumann, even before he damaged one of his fingers, was not a pianist of the calibre of Chopin; but the intimate character of much of his music suggests that their outlook on performance cannot have been very dissimilar.

All in all, therefore, it would seem advisable for today's interpreter of Chopin and Schumann to moderate the power of his instrument somewhat. The impression of strength and weight of tone must often be there; but there should always be a reserve, to match not only both composers' preference for an intimate atmosphere, but also the 'inward' quality that is such an essential part of their music.

The full dynamic range of the modern piano was available to Liszt and Brahms. Brahms must have written for just such an instrument from a fairly early age. And though Liszt belonged to the previous generation, his music, like that of Beethoven, always demanded and anticipated every increase in power that the piano manufacturer could supply. Moreover, he outlived his contemporaries Chopin and Schumann by many years; so for much of his career he was able to play on the modern piano itself.

PEDALLING

Since keyboard instruments prior to the fortepiano had no sustaining pedal, it is essential to avoid the anachronistic use of the pedal when playing early music on the piano. The sustaining pedal can provide an invaluable extension of the piano's range of colour; but in doing so it must never be allowed to produce the sort of effect that belongs exclusively to a later type of music. For example, if the figure appeared in the left hand part of a piece of 19th-century piano music, it is more than likely the composer would have intended all five notes to be held throughout the bar by means of the pedal. A harpsichord composer, on the other hand, would never have intended such an effect, for the simple reason that it was impossible on the instrument for which

he was writing. He might have wanted anything between

and ; but with a single hand he could not possibly have

sustained the first three quavers into the second half of the bar. Hence it would be a mistake to use the pedal to do so on the piano, should such a passage occur in a harpsichord or clavichord work.

The safest way to find the proper use of the sustaining pedal in early music is to begin by playing a piece without any pedal at all. (The possibilities of the *tenuto* type of touch shown in the last example above should never be forgotten, for it is a most important resource in harpsichord and clavichord playing.) Having achieved the phrasing that the music demands, the player can then add any touches of pedal that may be required for purposes of colour, being careful neither to obscure nor contradict the phrasing he has already obtained. If he does this with care, he may be surprised at the number of pedal changes that are required—one on every semiquaver is by no means unusual; but he will be well on the way to mastering the type of pedalling that can be used without anachronism in the performance of early music.

The left-hand ('soft') pedal (Italian, *una corda*; French, *sourdine*; German, *Verschiebung*) is less of a problem. Since it affects nothing but the tone it can be used for long or short periods as required. The player must, however, be on his guard against relying on its help every time he wants to produce a quiet sound; otherwise he will halve the number of colours at his disposal, and (worse still) become incapable of appreciating and producing subtle tonal differences by the use of his fingers alone.

With music written for the fortepiano the difference in the effect of the sustaining pedal on old and modern instruments must also be borne in mind. Since the tone of the fortepiano was comparatively light and evanescent, the pedal could be held down unchanged for much longer than would be tolerable on the piano of today. This can be seen from the first movement of Haydn's late Sonata in C, Hob. XVI/50, first published *c.* 1800 in London, where we find the pedal left unchanged through four bars of conflicting harmonies:

On the fortepiano this would have produced a mysterious rather than a muddled effect; but the present-day pianist would be ill-advised to follow the directions literally. Instead, he should aim at achieving the intended effect with the means at his disposal: i.e. with the help of some discreet half-pedalling. Though this Sonata is the only work of Haydn that contains pedal marks, there is no reason to suppose that he wished the pedal to remain unused elsewhere. Mozart showed the liveliest interest in the pedal-mechanism on Stein's pianos and was obviously accustomed to using it; yet there is not a single pedal indication in his music. Doubtless both composers took every advantage of an effect which is so integral a part of the instrument, but omitted the indications from their scores—with the exception of the single Haydn Sonata—because the effect of the pedal varied so much from one instrument to another that it was safer to leave its use to the musicianship of the performer. It may be said in general that the music of Haydn and Mozart demands frequent and unobtrusive changes of pedal, so that the characteristic clarity of its texture is never obscured.

Pedal indications appear more often in the music of Clementi and Beethoven. Yet here again it must be remembered that only the most essential or unusual are marked, and that these sometimes require less literal than idiomatic translation into terms of the modern piano. An extreme case is the first movement of the so-called 'Moonlight' Sonata, Op. 27/2, where Beethoven instructs the player twice, in case there should be any misunderstanding, that the whole movement is to be played *senʒa sordini* (without dampers)—that is, with the r.h. pedal held down unchanged from beginning to end. This effect cannot be reproduced exactly on a modern piano, as the result would be hopelessly muddled; but if the instrument possesses a third pedal, we can approximate fairly closely to it by the following device. Before the movement is begun, all the notes on the keyboard *below* E₁ sharp (the lowest note in the piece) are depressed silently and 'caught' by the middle pedal, which is kept down by the left foot throughout the movement. The r.h. pedal is then used in the normal way, and changed as the harmony dictates. This allows the undamped lowest strings to act as sympathetic resonators, so that they vibrate continuously and produce a faint but perceptible haze of sound from beginning to end, through which the cantabile of the r.h. can sound, as Beethoven himself put it, 'like a voice from a vault'.

At times this effect can be achieved without the help of a third pedal. If the passage happens to be confined to the r.h.—as it is towards the end of the slow movement of Beethoven's Piano Concerto No. 2 in B flat (bb.74–83), or during the two *Largo* recitatives in the first movement of his Sonata in D minor, Op. 31/2 (bb.143 and 153)—the l.h. can be used to depress silently and hold down a thick handful of notes in the extreme bass. The undamped strings of these notes will then act as resonators in exactly the same way as the notes caught by the third pedal.

But even if a third pedal is available and appropriate, it must be used with care; for if any of the 'caught' notes have to be restruck, there is always a tendency for them to sound disproportionately loud. (This is the reason in the 'Moonlight' Sonata for holding down only those notes that lie below the compass of the piece.) Thus if the third pedal is used in Beethoven's Bagatelle in E flat, Op. 126/3 (*S & I* III, p. 54) the last four E flats in the bass and the l.h. G in b.50 must all be played delicately, as they form part of the chord on the 1st beat of b.48 that was 'caught' by the pedal.

When the context makes it inadvisable or impossible to use the third pedal, or, as often happens, the piano does not possess one, the player must do as best he can with the means at his disposal. Occasionally it may be possible to follow the directions literally—Schnabel always did this—by playing with extreme delicacy; but more often it will be found wise to try and achieve the desired effect with the help of the kind of half-pedalling that allows a faint haze of sound to remain, yet prevents too great a clash between adjacent conflicting harmonies.

The use of the l.h. ('soft') pedal presents fewer problems, for its effect on early and modern instruments is more nearly similar. Neither Haydn nor Mozart indicates it in his scores; but both are likely to have been familiar with the effect and to have used it, for the mechanism, either in the form of a hand-stop, a device worked by the knee, or a pedal, was quite normal on fortepianos ever since its invention by Christofori in 1726.

Beethoven in the slow movement of his Sonata in A, Op. 101 specifies the use of the l.h. pedal by means of the German and Italian words *Mit einer Saite: Sul una corda* (on one string); and cancels it with the words *Alle Saiten: tutto il Cembalo* (all strings). But since his was a true *una corda* mechanism, which enabled one, two, or all three strings of each note to be struck by the hammer, he was able to introduce an intermediate step, *Nach und nach mehrere Saiten* (gradually more strings). This effect cannot be imitated on a modern piano, as the mechanism only shifts the action sufficiently to make the hammers strike two of the three strings.

Schubert indicates the l.h. pedal by the word *sordini* (mutes) in the slow movement of his Sonata in A minor, Op. 143, and elsewhere. It should be remembered that this has nothing to do with Beethoven's mark *senza sordini*, which means without dampers and refers to the use of the r.h. pedal.

The Romantic period might almost be called the Era of the Sustaining Pedal. It would be perfectly possible, though hardly comfortable, to give a musical performance of Haydn's or Mozart's complete keyboard works without touching the pedals. But almost every piece by a Romantic composer depends at one point or another, and sometimes throughout, on the use of the sustaining pedal.

The fundamental cause of this change was the gradually increasing sonority of the piano itself. With the greatly enriched harmonics of the newer instruments, 'close-position' chords in the bass, whether broken or unbroken, no longer sounded tolerable. Composers therefore opened out the chords, played their notes successively instead of simultaneously, and used the pedal to sustain what could not be stretched by a single hand. This was only a development of an age-old device, for broken chords had been used from an early time to provide both rhythmic interest and a sustaining effect in keyboard music. What was new was the realization that the pedal permitted spacings which were not only beyond the reach of a single hand, but also peculiarly suited to the evanescent tone of the piano. New and beautiful keyboard textures were thus evolved, whose immense potentialities were developed continuously up to the time of Debussy and beyond. Two basic types may be distinguished. In the first, the chord is spread out in single notes, as in Field's Nocturne No. 5 (*S & I* IV, p. 17), where

represents

And in the second, the chord is divided into smaller chords, or a combination of smaller chords and single notes, such as are found in Chopin's Mazurka in C sharp minor, Op. 50/3 (*S & I* IV, p. 28), where

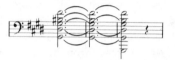

represents

It is important that such lay-outs, and any combination of them, should be recognized by the player, for though they depend entirely on the r.h. pedal for their effect, the composer (as can be seen from the first example) does not always bother to mark the necessary pedal changes in his score. When there are no marks, the safest way to determine the pedalling is to reduce the open-textured 'chords' to their closed position, as shown in the 2nd half of the above examples. The pedalling will then generally be found to coincide with the changes of harmony. At times, of course, other factors must be taken into consideration. In Brahms's Capriccio in C, Op. 76/8 (*S & I* IV, p. 52), the first three bars contain only two basic harmonies each; yet three pedals per bar will probably be required—on the 1st, 5th, and 9th quavers—otherwise the middle of each bar may sound over-thick. But notice that the second pedal-change, on the 5th quaver, never involves the loss of the true bass, for the 5th note is always just an octave higher than the 1st. In bb.49–50, on the contrary, the pedal could not be changed on the 5th quavers, as this would mean losing the true bass. Instead, the passage must be pedalled thus:

Another possible reason for modifying 'harmonic' pedalling may be the complexity of the r.h. part. The lesser sustaining power of the treble as compared with the bass will generally take care of this. But at times the sound must be thinned out by means of the kind of half-pedalling that leaves the more resonant bass notes still partly audible; and in extreme cases the bass must be abandoned altogether and left to the surprisingly co-operative imagination of the listener.

In the Brahms example above, the editorial marks in brackets indicate legato-pedalling, the type most frequently used nowadays. Here, the pedal is depressed immediately *after* a note has been struck, and released simultaneously with the attack on a note; with the result that the second note is joined to the first in a perfect legato, and without the slightest trace of 'fuzz' or carry-over in sound from one to the other. An earlier method, now less often used, is sometimes known as rhythmic-pedalling. Here the pedal is depressed *simultaneously* with the attack, and released just before a note is struck. The legato obtained thus may be slightly less perfect; but the notes acquired a sort of 'bloom', due to the sympathetic vibration of the other undamped strings, which can be extremely beautiful in a slow cantabile. A third type of pedalling, related to the last, can only be used after a silence. In it, the pedal is depressed *before* the note is struck, with results very similar to those achieved by rhythmic-pedalling.

The editorial pedal-marks shown above, and several other types found in 20th-century editions, can give absolutely precise indications of pedalling. Unfortunately, the same cannot be said of the normal 19th-century marks, *Ped* and ⁂. Not only are these too large to be exact, but they were often written and printed very haphazardly. Generally this was due to sheer carelessness; but at times it was because there was not enough space in either the MS or the engraving to place the signs correctly. This is particularly true of the bulky *Ped* sign, which often gets pushed to one side by the ledger-lines of the bass note to which it is meant to apply.

These various facts, coupled with the previously mentioned difference in sonority between old and modern instruments, all suggest that pedal indications in romantic music, as in classical, should be interpreted with discretion rather than followed blindly. The player should do his best to divine what effect the composer was aiming at in each instance. He should then strive to reproduce that effect as closely as possible with the means at his disposal.

One other notational peculiarity connected with the sustaining pedal must be mentioned. As can be seen from the Chopin example quoted above, composers sometimes use staccato marks in combination with pedal signs. At first sight this would appear to be a contradiction in terms. What is meant, however, is not that the player should attempt an impossible shortening of the notes concerned, but that he should play them with the same touch and attack as he would use for a staccato; for this, as experiment will show, produces a slightly different tone from playing the same notes legato and with pedal.

LIMITATIONS OF COMPASS

One further difference between old and modern pianos occasionally poses problems of interpretation. It is caused by the gradual increase over the years in the compass of keyboards. Until about 1790 fortepianos generally had a compass of five octaves, from F_1 an octave below the bass stave to f''' an octave above the treble stave. Additional half-octaves were then gradually added, first at one end of the keyboard and then at the other, till a compass of seven octaves become normal for grand pianos by about 1840.

It is interesting to note in passing that Haydn's piano in 1765 must have had an incomplete bottom octave, with some system of 'short-octave' tuning. (See Chapter 1: The Instruments, p. 7.) This is shown by the last three l.h. chords in his Capriccio, Hob. XVII/1 (*S & I* III, p. 16), which in the original

autograph read:

Few hands could stretch this on a normally tuned keyboard; but with short-octave tuning it would only involve the stretch of an octave. It is significant, however, that the chord was altered to a plain G octave in the first printed edition of 1788.

The gradual enlargement of keyboards took place at different times in different countries; but the important thing to notice is the effect that the changes had on various composers. Mozart restricted his keyboard writing to the compass of five octaves from F_1 to f''', and showed such ingenuity in so doing that the listener is never aware of any sense of limitation. As a rule Haydn did likewise; but in his late Sonata in C, Hob. XVI/50, published *c.* 1800, he extended the compass upwards by a third to a''', possibly because the work was intended for England, where piano makers had enlarged their keyboards earlier than elsewhere. Beethoven kept within the early five-octave compass in his works up to and including the 'Kreutzer' Sonata, Op. 47, for violin and piano, which was completed in 1802 and published in 1805. But the Piano Concerto No. 3 in C minor, Op. 37, is an exception; for though the work was written in 1800, Beethoven revised the piano part to include the upward extension of a fifth before it was published in 1804. This compass of five octaves and a fifth, from bass F_1 to treble c'''', was not exceeded in any of the piano Sonatas until the A major, Op. 101, which required six octaves from E_1 to e''''. Finally, from the time of the 'Hammerklavier' Sonata, Op. 106, Beethoven wrote his piano works for a keyboard of six and a half octaves from C_1 to f''''.

The significance of these changes is that composers did not always manage, like Mozart, to hide the fact that they were hampered by restrictions of compass. The question thus arises: should a performer play what composers found themselves forced to write, or should he substitute what they probably would have written had they possessed a larger keyboard?

The problem is well illustrated by a passage from the opening Andante of Clementi's Sonata in D, Op. 10/2 (*S & I* III, p. 29), where it is evident from bb.64–66 of the revised autograph that Clementi's piano went up to a''' a tenth above the treble stave. Yet because the normal domestic instrument of the period ended at f''', a third lower, the composer felt obliged in the earlier printed version to write:

This is so obviously a second-best that there can be no doubt about preferring the revision. But we might go still further: for even if the autograph were unknown, the player would have good reason for continuing the octave figure in b.66 right up to a''', and thus carrying on Clementi's already established pattern, for this would be so much more musical than his rather lame alternative.

Similarly, in the first movement of Beethoven's Sonata in D, Op. 10/3, it might be legitimate to continue the quaver figure established in b.102 up to a''' in b.105, instead of letting it settle on e''' in b.104, as printed in the score.

The distortion of a phrase through restrictions of compass can equally well occur in the bass. In the slow movement of Beethoven's early Sonata in C, Op. 2/3, the second theme (b.11) consists in the l.h. of pairs of crotchet octaves slowly mounting in thirds. Later, in b.26, when this figure appears at a lower pitch, the lack of an E͵ has forced Beethoven to change the first rising

third into a falling sixth:  . As no musical purpose is

served by this alteration, and as it greatly minimizes the effect of the sudden *ff*, the performer would be well advised to emend the passage, this time by transposing the Es down an octave.

There is a curious passage in the first movement of the Sonata in A, Op. 101, which should also be noted. In b.24 the shape of the r.h. arpeggio would lead one to suppose that the parallel passage in b.76 had been altered because the high c'''' sharp and e'''' were missing on Beethoven's piano. Yet, oddly enough, in bb.77–78 of the last movement there is a scale that goes all the way up to this very e''''. Beethoven could therefore have used the original form of the arpeggio in b.76 of the first movement if he had wished; and since he did not do so, the passage should be left as it stands.

Another passage that was altered in recapitulation, yet should not be emended, is found in the first movement of the Sonata in D minor, Op. 31/2. At b.59 of the exposition, part of the second subject group appears thus:

When this theme is recapitulated in the tonic at b.189 Beethoven has had to alter the layout, to avoid overstepping the f''' which was then the upper limit of his keyboard:

Yet this new version is in itself so striking, and, with its insistent inverted pedal on D, so much more intense than the original, that there can be no question of emending it into a plain transposition.

Schubert's piano had a compass of six octaves from F_1 to f'''', and the downward limit is sometimes so awkwardly apparent that it is wise to supply the notes that had to be omitted.

How, then, is the player to decide whether he should or should not emend a passage that is quite clearly the result of a limitation in the compass of the composer's keyboard? The answer is fairly straightforward. If the composer has made musical capital out of his alteration, by bringing to light some imaginative, new, or unexpected aspect of the material, his own version should be left as it stands. If, on the other hand, he has merely accepted the limitation as a tiresome necessity, and provided no more than an obviously second-best alternative, it may then be better to play what the composer would probably have written had the requisite notes been available. One proviso must be made, however. The emended version should never introduce a totally alien tone-colour or exceed too noticeably the prevailing tessitura of the piece, otherwise it will make itself uncomfortably obtrusive and strike the listener as disturbing rather than natural.

Further Reading

(See the following in Suggestions for Further Reading, pp. 177 ff.)

Badura-Skoda, Eva and Paul, *Interpreting Mozart on the Keyboard*.
Riefling, Riemar, *Piano Pedalling*.

10 Editors' Problems

THE EDITOR'S TASK

By way of epilogue some facts concerning editions and editing in general may be briefly considered. If their relevance to performance is not immediately obvious it will soon become apparent.

In the first place it must be remembered that few musical texts can be printed exactly as they stand. Even a composer's autograph may be full of mistakes and ambiguities which must be corrected or resolved before it can be handed over to an engraver. (Among recent composers Bartók and Stravinsky were exceptional in this respect, for they knew and indicated precisely how their works should appear on the printed page.) If the source of a text is not an autograph, but either a MS copy or an early printed edition, it is likely to be even less reliable; for copyists and engravers are as fallible as other human beings (composers and editors included), while some are grossly careless and others are plain muddle-headed.

In addition, a work sometimes occurs in more than a single source. Thus there may be several autographs all differing from one another, and here it must be decided which provides the most satisfactory text. (A composer's second thoughts are not necessarily his best—for example Schumann's; but a player should generally be allowed to see them.) Alternatively, an autograph may exist together with a contemporary printed edition or a MS in another hand, or several of each; and if this is so, it is not always the autograph that will provide the definitive text, for the composer may have made important alterations at the proof stage; or the MS could be a copy of a later autograph version that has since disappeared. Finally, no autograph whatever may have survived (as with Scarlatti's 555 Sonatas), in which case the text must be supplied from whatever early editions or MS copies are available.

In all these instances an editor's intervention is required in order to establish the text itself. Less obviously, it may also be needed in order to make the original readable by the player of today; for the further we move back in time the more unfamiliar the notation is likely to be. During the pre-classical period, for example, the following six systems of notating keyboard music were in use in one place or another:

1. Mensural notation on two staves. This was closest to the system used today, though the staves (particularly the upper one) often had more than five lines apiece. In Italy it was known as *intavolatura*.

2. Mensural notation in open score, i.e. with a separate 5-line stave for each contrapuntal part. Known in Italy as *in partitura*, this was specially useful for study purposes since it gave such a clear picture of the part-writing (e.g. Frescobaldi's *Il primo libro di capricci...*, 1624, and Bach's *Die Kunst der Fuge*, 1752). It also had the advantage of being easy to engrave or set up in type.

3. Mensural notation with each contrapuntal part in a separate part-book. This was used for works intended *per sonare con ogni sorte di stromenti*—'to be played on any instruments' (e.g. G. Gabrieli's *Canzoni... 1608*). It was inconvenient for the keyboard player since it required him to write out his own performing copy, but practical both for the publisher and for ensemble players.

4. Old German Keyboard Tablature, current in Germany during the 15th and 16th centuries. Here the top part was written in mensural notation on a single stave of from 5 to 8 lines, while the remaining parts were shown by letters of the alphabet (A to G, with different sized letters and/or diacritical marks to indicate the octave required), and, where necessary, rhythmic symbols (e.g. the *Buxheimer Orgelbuch, c. 1575*).

5. New German Keyboard Tablature, used in Germany from the late 16th to the late 18th century. Here all the parts were shown by letters of the alphabet (A to G, with different sized letters and/or diacritical marks to indicate the octave required), and, where necessary, rhythmic symbols (e.g. Ammerbach's *Orgel oder Instrument Tabulatur*, 1571). From the printer's point of view this was simpler than any of the foregoing systems, since it involved neither notes nor staves and was economical of space. Bach used it in order to squeeze in an extra line at the foot of some pages of the autograph of his *Orgelbüchlein*, 1717–23.

6. Spanish Keyboard Tablature, current in Spain in the 16th century. Here all the parts were shown by numerals and, where necessary, rhythmic symbols. The numerals used were either 1 to 42, representing the chromatic compass of the keyboard from C to a″, with a short-octave bass (e.g. Bermudo's *Declaración de instrumentes musicales*, 1555); or else 1 to 7, representing the white-note scale of F to E, with diacritical marks to indicate the octave required, and

sharps and flats to show chromatic alteration (e.g. Cabezón's *Obras de música,* 1578).

In addition to bringing these unfamiliar notational systems into line with present-day practice, an editor must often make other adjustments in order to provide an easily intelligible text: for the average player would be baffled by, say, the 16th- and 17th-century habit of placing G-, F-, and C-clefs on whichever line happened to be convenient; and he might even be puzzled by the way in which composers as unexotic as Mozart, Beethoven, Schubert, and Chopin may or may not expect an accidental to carry over into subsequent bars or different octaves. Such adjustments can generally be made without fear of misrepresenting the composer's intentions; but a conscientious editor will always differentiate clearly, either typographically or by means of textual notes, between what actually appears in the original source and what he himself has added or emended.

MISREADINGS AND MISPRINTS

It should nevertheless be remembered that even the most careful editor can nod, and that the best-intentioned editions can contain misreadings, never to mention mere misprints. In the original source of the *Fitzwilliam Virginal Book,* for example, there are wrong notes and even missing bars that remain uncorrected in the modern complete edition. And in Couperin's harpsichord piece, 'Les Tours de Passe-passe', Ordre 22, the Brahms & Chrysander edition prints one hand a 3rd too low—making harmonic nonsense—in 27 out of its 77 bars, simply because a treble clef on the bottom line of the stave has been misread as a normal treble clef. Even modern 1st editions can be untrustworthy, for some composers seem incapable of reading proofs.

It is as well, therefore, to preserve a degree of scepticism concerning the absolute accuracy of any printed page. This does not mean that every passage that sounds in the least unusual is due to either a misprint or an editor's misreading. Composers must be allowed their surprises. But if a note or a passage, after repeated hearings, continues to sound foreign to its context and to the known style of the composer, it is then time to consider whether it is perhaps a mistake; and, if so, what *kind* of mistake. This last point is specially important, for it is essential to recognize the nature of a misprint or misreading before attempting to correct it, otherwise it is only too easy to substitute a new error for the old. Some of the commonest mistakes in both manuscript and printed music are the following: (a) an accidental omitted; (b) the wrong accidental used; (c) a note misplaced by one degree (e.g. D instead of either C or E); (d) a note misplaced by two degrees (e.g. D instead of either B or F); (e) the wrong clef used; (f) the dot of a dotted-note omitted; (g) an ornament omitted; (h) the wrong ornament used; (i) one line, or part of a line, omitted from a contrapuntal texture; (k) a bar or more omitted, specially when the first omitted chord is the same as the chord immediately following the omission; and (l) a bar or more duplicated.

When a doubtful passage could be the result of one of these common types of error, or of some other easily explainable cause, it is worth considering whether it should be emended. On the other hand, it is highly dangerous to make an emendation *in vacuo*, i.e. without being able to explain how the mistake could have arisen in the first place. Ideally speaking, emendations should be the concern of the editor alone; but, as we have seen, the player may find at times that he himself must do what the editor has left undone, or done wrongly.

URTEXTS AND OTHERS

It is only comparatively recently that publishers have begun to realize that reprints of older music, in other than library editions, should attempt to give an unencumbered picture of the composer's text. In the second half of the 19th century, when most of the standard German popular editions of the classics were first produced, it was usual to invite a famous virtuoso or teacher to act as editor. This he would do by smothering the text with his own marks of phrasing, dynamics, and fingering, none of which were in any way distinguishable from those of the composer. (An honourable exception was Dr. Hans Bischoff, whose Steingräber edition of the keyboard works of Bach, published in the 1880s and recently re-issued by Kalmus in America, clearly differentiated between Bach and Bischoff, and ingeniously managed at the same time to include most of the variant readings that were then known.)

In reaction to this approach, and as a corrective to some of the inadequately edited volumes of the great Collected Editions of Breitkopf & Härtel, the Berlin Academy of Arts began in the 1890s to issue a series of 'Urtexts' (original texts) of some of the keyboard works of J. S. Bach, C. P. E. Bach, Mozart, Beethoven, and Chopin. Their aim, not always successfully realized, was to present the composer's unadulterated text as it appeared in the most reliable autograph or early edition. Other German publishers slowly followed this lead, with the result that more and more 'Urtexts' appeared from the 1930s onwards. Sometimes the description was merited, and sometimes it was not.

One normally reputable publisher even fell as low as adding a new cover and title-page, prominently labelled *Urtext*, to a grossly over-edited volume that had been in his list for years. Luckily, however, this sort of thing was the exception rather than the rule; and in recent years firms have on the whole tackled with increasing seriousness the problem of providing reliable and scholarly editions for the student. The Henle Verlag and Bärenreiter Verlag in Germany, Heugel in France, and Stainer & Bell and the Oxford University Press in England provide notable examples of this trend.

Yet in spite of the gradual improvement in standards of editing, bad editions of every description still abound. For this reason a student should take careful thought before laying the all-important foundations of his working library, otherwise much of his money may be wasted. He might find that Beethoven's views on the dynamics of Bach, as reported in Czerny's edition of The Forty-Eight Preludes & Fugues, have a certain interest of their own; but they do not provide a very satisfactory basis on which to build an authentic interpretation. Nor do many other editions that are swamped in arbitrary editorial markings.

If the student keeps his eyes open he will gradually learn to recognize the outward signs of a good or a bad edition. Until he can do this, he may find it helpful to remember the following points:

1. In an edition of music of an earlier period, the source or sources of the text should always be stated.

2. There should be some form of editorial commentary, however short, which presents the relevant facts concerning the work and its editing.

3. Editorial marks should be differentiated typographically from those of the original.

4. Significant editorial alterations of the text should be noted.

5. When editorial realizations of ornaments or rhythmic conventions have been added, they should *not* be incorporated in the text, but printed separately above or below the stave, or at the foot of the page.

The fulfilment of these conditions is no guarantee of the quality of the editing itself; but they are the minimum requirements that should be expected of any modern edition that claims to be worthy of serious consideration.

Further Reading

(See the following in Suggestions for Further Reading, pp. 177 ff.)

Emery, Walter, *Editions and Musicians.*
Grove's Dictionary, under Notation.

11 Suggestions for Further Reading

Apel, Willi, *Masters of the Keyboard*; Harvard Univ. Press, Cambridge 1947.

Apel, Willi, *The Notation of Polyphonic Music 900–1600*; Mediaeval Academy of America, Cambridge 1953 (4th ed.).

Apel, Willi, *Geschichte der Orgel- und Klaviermusik bis 1700*; Bärenreiter, Kassel 1967. English trans. by Hans Tischler, *The History of Keyboard Music to 1700*; Indiana Univ. Press, Bloomington 1972.

Arbeau, Thoinot, *Orchésographie*, c. 1589, trans. Mary Stewart Evans; Dover Publications, New York 1967. Concerning French dances.

Bach, Carl Philipp Emanuel, *Versuch über die wahre Art das Clavier zu spielen*, 1752/62. English trans. by William J. Mitchell, *Essay on the True Art of Playing Keyboard Instruments*; Cassell, London 1951 (2nd ed.).

Bach, Johann Sebastian, *Forty-Eight Preludes and Fugues*, i–ii, ed. Donald Francis Tovey; Associated Board, London 1924. Includes invaluable notes on each work.

Bach, Johann Sebastian, *The 'Goldberg' Variations*, ed. Ralph Kirkpatrick; Schirmer, New York 1938. Includes an invaluable preface.

Badura-Skoda, Eva and Paul, *Interpreting Mozart on the Keyboard*; Barrie & Rockliff, London 1962.

Beethoven, Ludwig van, *Pianoforte Sonatas* 1–3, ed. with commentaries by Donald Francis Tovey; Associated Board, London 1931. *A Companion to Beethoven's Pianoforte Sonatas*, containing a bar-by-bar analysis, by Donald Francis Tovey; Associated Board, London 1931.

Boalch, Donald Howard, *Makers of the Harpsichord and Clavichord 1440–1840*; Ronald, London 1956. (2nd ed., Clarendon Press, Oxford 1974.)

Borrel, Eugène, *L'Interpretation de la musique française de Lully à la Révolution*; Alcan, Paris 1934.

Borren, Charles van den, *The Sources of Keyboard Music in England*; Novello, London [1913].

Caldwell, John, *English Keyboard Music before the 19th Century*; Blackwell, Oxford 1973.

Clutton, Cecil, 'Arnault's MS', *The Galpin Society Journal* v, March 1952.

Couperin, François, *L'Art de toucher le clavecin*, 1716/17, ed. in French, German, and

English by Anna Linde; Breitkopf & Härtel, Leipzig 1933.

Dale, Kathleen, *Nineteenth-Century Piano Music*; Oxford Univ. Press, London 1954.

Dannreuther, Edward, *Musical Ornamentation* i–ii; Novello, London [1893–95].

Dart, R. Thurston, *The Interpretation of Music*; Hutchinson, London 1954.

Davie, Cedric Thorpe, *Musical Structure and Design*; Dobson, London 1953. Paperback by Dover, New York.

Dolmetsch, Arnold, *The Interpretation of Music of the 17th and 18th Centuries*; Novello, London [1915]. A separately printed Appendix contains twenty-two pieces with many examples of early fingering.

Donington, Robert, *The Interpretation of Early Music*; Faber, London 1965 (2nd ed.). Deals comprehensively with the performance of music between, roughly, Monteverdi and J. S. Bach, and includes some 750 long quotations from contemporary authorities.

Dunn, John Petrie, *Ornamentation in the Works of Frederick Chopin*; Novello, London [1921].

Emery, Walter, *Bach's Ornaments*; Novello, London 1953. The clearest and most compact discussion of the subject.

Emery, Walter, *Editions and Musicians*; Novello, London 1957. A concise statement of the problems of editing.

Friskin, James, & Freundlich, Irwin, *Music for the Piano . . . 1580–1952*; Rinehart, New York 1954.

Geoffroy-Dechaume, Antoine, *Les 'Secrets' de la musique ancienne*; Fasquelle, Paris 1964.

Georgii, Walter, *Klaviermusik*; Atlantic, Zürich 1950 (2nd ed.).

Grove's Dictionary of Music and Musicians, i–ix, 5th ed.; Macmillan, London 1954. Specially the articles on Baroque interpretation, Dotted notes, Expression, Fingering (keyboard), Harpsichord, Hydraulis, Inégales, Notation, Organ, Ornamentation, Phrasing, and Pianoforte.

Harding, Rosamond E. M., *The Pianoforte: its History to . . . 1851*; Cambridge Univ. Press, Cambridge 1933.

Harding, Rosamond E. M., *Origins of Musical Time and Expression*; Oxford Univ. Press, London 1938.

Hinson, Maurice, *Guide to the Pianist's Repertoire*; Indiana Univ. Press, Bloomington 1973. Remarkably comprehensive 800-page volume, including early keyboard music, but not duets.

Keyboard Music, ed. Denis Matthews; Penguin Books, Harmondsworth 1972. Hardback ed: David & Charles, Newton Abbot, 1972. A handy guide from the 14th to the 20th century by seven writers.

Kirby, F. E., *A Short History of Keyboard Music*; The Free Press, New York 1966.

Kirkpatrick, Ralph, *Domenico Scarlatti*; Princeton Univ. Press, Princeton 1953. Includes an invaluable chapter on Scarlatti's ornamentation.

Mellers, Wilfrid H., *François Couperin and the French Classical Tradition*; Dobson, London 1950. Includes a useful discussion on *notes inégales*.

Merian, Wilhelm, *Der Tanz in den deutschen Tabulaturbüchern*; Breitkopf & Härtel, Leipzig 1916 (reprinted Olms 1968).

Morley, Thomas, *A Plaine and Easie Introduction to Practicall Musicke*, 1597, ed. R. Alec Harman; Dent, London 1952

Mozart, J. G. Leopold, *Versuch einer gründlichen Violinschule*, 1756. English trans. by Edith Knocker, *A Treatise on the Fundamental Principles of Violin Playing*; Oxford Univ. Press, London 1948. Of wider interest than the title would suggest.

Quantz, Johann Joachim, *Versuch einer Anweisung die Flöte traversiere zu spielen*, 1752. English trans. by Edward R. Reilly, *On Playing the Flute*; Faber, London 1966. Of wider interest than the title would suggest.

Rameau, Jean-Philippe, *Pièces de clavecin*, ed. Erwin R. Jacobi; Bärenreiter, Kassel 1958. Includes Rameau's own prefaces in French, German, and English.

Riefling, Riemar, *Piano Pedalling*; Oxford Univ. Press, London 1962.

Russell, Raymond, *The Harpsichord and Clavichord*; Faber, London 1973 (2nd ed.).

Sachs, Kurt, *Rhythm and Tempo*; Dent, London 1953.

Scarlatti, Domenico, *Sixty Sonatas*, ed. Ralph Kirkpatrick; Schirmer, New York 1953. Includes an invaluable preface.

Schmitz, Hans-Peter, *Die Kunst der Verzierung im 18. Jahrhundert*; Bärenreiter, Kassel 1955. Includes many full-length examples.

Schott, Howard, *The Harpsichord*; Faber, London 1973.

Stein, Erwin, *Form and Performance*; Faber, London 1962.

Stevens, Denis, *The Mulliner Book: a Commentary*; Stainer & Bell, London 1952.

Sumner, William L., *The Organ: its Evolution, Principles of Construction and Use*; Macdonald, London 1973 (4th ed.).

Tovey, Donald Francis, *A Companion to [Bach's] 'The Art of Fugue'*; Oxford Univ. Press, London 1931. A bar-by-bar analysis.

Tovey, Donald Francis, *Essays in Musical Analysis: Chamber Music*; Oxford Univ. Press, London 1944. Specially the articles on Bach's 'Goldberg' Variations, Beethoven's Diabelli Variations, and Brahms's Variations on the theme by Paganini.

Tovey, Donald Francis, *The Forms of Music*; Oxford Univ. Press, London 1944. Specially the articles on Contrapuntal forms, Fugue, Melody, Rondo, Scherzo, Sonata forms, and Variations.

Türk, Daniel Gottlob, *Klavierschule*, 1789. Facsimile ed. by Edwin R. Jacobi; Bärenreiter, Kassel 1962.

Westrup, Jack, *Musical Interpretation*; B.B.C., London 1971. A concise statement of the problems.

Wolters, Klaus, *Handbuch der Klavierliteratur*; Atlantis, Zürich 1967. The most comprehensive catalogue to date.

12 Some Modern Editions

FACSIMILES

of autographs, contemporary manuscripts, and early editions

Arne, Thomas Augustine
  VIII Sonatas or Lessons (1st ed.), ed. G. Beechey & T. Dart; Stainer & Bell, London 1960.
Attaingnant, Pierre
  Chansons und Tänze, 1–5 (1st ed.), ed. E. Bernoulli; Kühn, Munich 1914. The first seven books of keyboard music printed in France, published by Pierre Attaingnant of Paris in 1530/31.
Bach, Johann Sebastian
  Clavier-Büchlein vor Wilhelm Friedemann Bach, 1720 (part-autograph), ed. Ralph Kirkpatrick; Yale Univ. Press, New Haven 1959.
  Das wohltemperierte Clavier, Book I (autograph), ed. Karl-Heinz Köhler; Deutscher Verlag für Musik, Leipzig 1962.
  Inventionen und Sinfonien (autograph), ed. Ralph Kirkpatrick; Peters, New York 1948. Also in paperback ed. Eric Simon; Dover, New York.
Beethoven, Ludwig van
  Sonata in A flat, Op. 26 (autograph); Beethovenhaus, Bonn 1894.
  Sonata in C sharp minor, Op. 27/2 (autograph); Universal, Vienna 1922.
  Sonata in C, Op. 53 (autograph); Beethovenhaus, Bonn 1964.
  Sonata in F minor, Op. 57 (autograph); H. Pizza, Paris [1927].
  Sonata in F sharp, Op. 78 (autograph); Drei Masken Verlag, Munich 1923.
  Sonata in E, Op. 109 (autograph); Lehman Foundation, Washington 1965.
  Sonata in A flat, Op. 110 (autograph); Ichthys Verlag, Stuttgart 1967.
  Sonata in C minor, Op. 111 (autograph); Drei Masken Verlag, Munich 1922. Also in paperback, ed. Eric Simon; Dover, New York.
Boyce, William
  Ten Voluntaries for the Organ or Harpsichord, c. 1785 (1st ed.), ed. John Caldwell; Oxford Univ. Press, London 1972.
Brahms, Johannes
  Variations & Fugue on a Theme by Handel, Op. 24, and *Variations on a Theme by*

Schumann for piano duet, Op. 23 (autograph): in a volume of Brahms facsimiles; Lehman Foundation, Washington 1967.

Buxheimer Orgelbuch (MS), ed. Bertha Antonia Wallner; Bärenreiter, Kassel 1955. The largest German anthology of early keyboard music; written in Old German Keyboard Tablature.

Chambonnières, Jacques Champion de
  Les Pièces de clauessin, 1 & 2, 1670 (1st ed.); Broude, New York.

Chopin, Frédéric François
  Ballade in F, Op. 36 (autograph)
  Ballade in A flat, Op. 47 (autograph)
  Barcarolle, Op. 60 (autograph)
  Etude in C minor, Op. 10/12 (autograph)
  Fantasie, Op. 49 (autograph)   ed. Wladyslaw Hordyński;
  Krakowiak, Op. 14 (autograph)   Polskie Wydawnictwo
  24 Préludes, Op. 28 (autograph)   Muzyczne, Cracow.
  Scherzo in B flat minor, Op. 31 (autograph)
  Scherzo in E, Op. 54 (autograph)
  Sonata in B minor, Op. 58 (autograph)
  Variations on 'La ci darem', Op. 2 (autograph)
  Etude in E, Op. 10/3 (autograph); Lehman Foundation, Washington 1964.
  Tarentelle, Op. 43 (autograph); Catin, Paris 1930.

Couperin, François
  Pièces de clavecin, 1713 (1st ed.)
  Second Livre de pièces de clavecin, 1717 (1st ed.)   (In preparation)
  Troisième Livre de pièces de clavecin, 1722 (1st ed.)   Broude, New York.
  Quatrième Livre de pièces de clavecin, 1730 (1st ed.)
  L'Art de toucher le clavecin, 1716/17 (1st & 2nd eds.); Broude, New York.

D'Anglebert, Jean Henry
  Pièces de clavecin, 1689 (1st ed.); Broude, New York.

Daquin, Louis-Claude
  Premier Livre de pièces de clavecin, 1735 (1st ed.); (In preparation) Broude, New York

Frescobaldi, Girolamo
  Ricercari e canzoni, 1615 (1st ed.); Gregg, Farnborough 1967. Printed in open score.

Giustini, Ludovico
  12 Pianoforte Sonatas, 1732 (1st ed.), ed. Rosamond E. M. Harding; Cambridge Univ. Press, Cambridge 1933. The earliest printed piano sonatas.

Haydn, Joseph
  Sonata in A, Hob. XVI/26 (autograph); Drei Masken Verlag, Munich 1928.

Ileborgh, Adam
> *Die Orgeltabulatur*, 1448 (autograph), ed. G. Most: Altmärkisch Museum, Stendal 1954. Written in Old German Keyboard Tablature.

Johannes de Lublin
> *Tabulatura*, c. 1537–c. 1548 (autograph): *Monumenta Musicae in Polonia*, Seria B/1; Polskie Wydawnictwo Muzyczne, Cracow 1964. The largest Polish collection of early keyboard music; written in Old German Keyboard Tablature.

Locke, Matthew
> *Melothesia*, 1673 (1st ed.); (In preparation) Broude, New York.

Mattheson, Johann
> *Pièces de clavecin*, 1714 (1st ed.); Broude, New York.

Mozart, Wolfgang Amadeus
> *Rondo in D*, K.485 and *Rondo in A minor*, K.511 (autograph), ed. Hans Gál; Universal, Vienna 1923. *Rondo in A minor*, K.511 (autograph); Peters, Leipzig c. 1955.

Muffat, Gottlieb
> *Componimenti musicali*, c. 1739 (1st ed.); Broude, New York.

Parthenia, [1612/13] (1st ed.), ed. Otto Erich Deutsch: *Harrow Replicas*, 3; Heffer, Cambridge 1942. 21 pieces by Byrd, Bull, and Gibbons: 'the first musicke that euer was printed for the virginalls'.

Parthenia In-Violata, c. 1620–29 (1st ed.), ed. Thurston Dart and others; New York Public Library, New York 1961. 20 English pieces for virginals and bass viol, the latter optional.

Paumann, Conrad
> *Fundamentum Organisandi*, 1452 (MS), ed. Konrad Ameln; Berlin 1925.

Picchi, Giovanni
> *Intavolatura di balli d'arpicordo*, 1621 (1st ed.): *Collezione di trattati e musiche antiche in fac-simile*; Bolletino Bibliografico Musicale, Milan 1934.

Purcell, Henry
> *A choice Collection of Lessons*, 1696 (1st ed.); Broude, New York.

Robertsbridge Fragment, c. 1320 (British Library, Add. MS 28550): plates 42–45 in H. E. Wooldridge's *Early English Harmony*; Plainsong and Mediaeval Music Society, Oxford 1897. This incomplete 2-leaf MS from the former priory of Robertsbridge in Sussex contains the earliest known keyboard music; written in Old German Keyboard Tablature.

Radino, Giovanni
> *Il primo libro d'intavolatura di balli d'arpicordo*, 1592 (1st ed.), ed. Rosamund E. M. Harding; Heffer, Cambridge 1949.

Rameau, Jean-Philippe
> *Pièces de clavecin*, 1724 (1st ed.); Broude, New York.
> *Nouvelle Suite de pièces de clavecin*, c. 1728 (1st ed.); Broude, New York.

Roseingrave, Thomas
  Eight Suits of Lessons, c. 1728 (1st ed.); Broude, New York.
Scarlatti, Domenico
  Complete Keyboard Works, 1–18 (MSS), ed. Ralph Kirkpatrick; Johnson, New York 1972 (mainly from the Parma MSS).
  Essercizi per gravicembalo, 1739 (1st ed.); Gregg, Farnborough 1967. Also included in the above.
Schmid, Bernard, the Younger
  Tabulatur Buch, 1607 (1st ed.); Broude, New York. Printed in New German Keyboard Tablature.
Schubert, Franz
  Unfinished sketch for the slow movement of Sonata in D flat, D.567 (autograph): *Harrow Replicas,* 1; Heffer, Cambridge 1943.
Schumann, Robert
  Jugend-Album, Op. 68 (mainly autograph), ed. Georg Eismann; Peters, Leipzig 1955.

ANTHOLOGIES

Anne Cromwell's Virginal Book, 1638, ed. Howard Ferguson; Oxford Univ. Press, London 1974.
Apel, Willi, *Keyboard Music of the 14th and 15th centuries: CEKM,* 1; American Institute of Musicology, 1963. Contains the earliest known keyboard music, the *Robertsbridge Fragment, c.* 1320; also Ileborgh's *Tabulatur,* 1448, Paumann's *Fundamentum organisandi,* 1452, and other early sources. See also Facsimiles, above.
Attaingnant, Pierre. The seven books of keyboard pieces published by Pierre Attaingnant of Paris in 1530/31 are available as follows: Vols. 1–3 (Chansons) in *Transcriptions of Chansons for Keyboard,* ed. Albert Seay; American Institute of Musicology, 1941. Vol. 4 (Dances) in *Keyboard Dances from the early 16th Century,* ed. Daniel Heartz; American Institute of Musicology, 1965. Vols. 5–6 (Mass-movements, Magnificats, etc.) and Vol. 7 (Motets) in, respectively, *Deux Livres d'orgue* and *Treize Motets et un prélude pour orgue,* ed. Yvonne Rokseth; Société Française de Musicologie, Paris 1925/30. See also Facsimiles, above.
Buxheimer Orgelbuch, ed. Bertha Antonia Wallner: *Das Erbe deutscher Musik,* 37–39; Bärenreiter, Kassel 1958. The largest German anthology of early keyboard music. See also Facsimiles, above.
Clement Matchett's Virginal Book, 1612, ed. Thurston Dart; Stainer & Bell, London 1957.

Curtis, Alan, *Dutch Keyboard Music of the 16th & 17th centuries*: *Monumenta Musica Neerlandica*, 3; Vereniging voor Nederlandse Musiekgeschiedenis, Amsterdam 1961. Contains the Susanne van Soldt MS complete, and some lesser MSS.

Dawes, Frank, *Early Keyboard Music*, 1; Schott, London 1951. Contains the ten pieces by Hugh Aston and anon. from British Library, MS Royal App. 58.

Diémer, Louis, *Les Clavecinistes français*, 1–4; Durand, Paris [n.d.]. A good selection; but over-edited, with ornament realizations incorporated in the text.

Dublin Virginal Manuscript, The, c. 1570, ed. John Ward: *The Wellesly Edition*, 3; Wellesly College, 1954.

Early Tudor Organ Music, 1–2: 1, Music for the Office, ed. John Caldwell; 2, Music for the Mass, ed. Denis Stevens: *Early English Church Music*, 6 & 10; Stainer & Bell, London 1966/69.

Elizabeth Roger's Virginal Book, 1656, ed. George Sargent: *CEKM*, 19; American Institute of Musicology, 1971.

Elliott, Kenneth, *Early Scottish Keyboard Music*; Stainer & Bell, London 1958.

Farrenc, Aristide & Louise, *Le Trésor des pianistes*, 1–23; Prilipp, Paris 1861–72. The most comprehensive anthology of 16th- to mid-19th-century keyboard music. Reprint announced by Broude, New York.

Ferguson, Howard, *Style and Interpretation*, 1–6. 1, Early keyboard music I (England & France); 2, Early keyboard music II (Italy & Germany); 3, Classical piano music; 4, Romantic piano music; 5, Keyboard duets I (17th & 18th centuries); 6, Keyboard duets II (19th & 20th centuries). Sequels to Vols 1 and 2 of the above: *Early English Keyboard Music*, 1–2; *Early French Keyboard Music*, 1–2; *Early Italian Keyboard Music*, 1–2; *Early German Keyboard Music*, 1–2. All published by the Oxford Univ. Press, London 1962–71. These volumes provide clean texts and include comprehensive introductions and notes regarding interpretation. They contain many of the pieces mentioned in the present book.

Fischer, Hans, and Oberdörffer, Fritz, *Deutsche Klaviermusik des 17. und 18. Jahrhunderts*, 1–9; Vieweg, Berlin-Lichterfelde 1960. Fairly easy pieces.

Fitzwilliam Virginal Book, The, ed. J. A. Fuller Maitland & W. Barclay Squire; Breitkopf & Härtel, Leipzig 1899. Excellent paperback by Dover, New York. The largest English anthology of virginals music.

Fuller Maitland, J. A., *The Contemporaries of Purcell*, 1–7; Chester, London 1921–22. A good selection from Blow, Clark, Croft, etc.; but over-edited, with ornament realizations incorporated in the text.

Guilmant, Alexander, *Archives des maîtres d'orgue des 16e–18e siècles*, 1–10; Schott, Mainz 1898–1907. Titelouze, Raison, Marchand, Clérambault, Du Mage, Daquin, Gigault, de Grigny, Boyvin, Dandrieu, Guilain, Scherer, Lebégue.

Intabolatura nova de varie sorte de balli, 1551: reprinted complete as *Intabolatura nova de balli*, ed. W. Oxenbury & T. Dart; Stainer & Bell, London 1965.

Jeppesen, Knud, *Balli antichi veneҳiani*; Hansen, Copenhagen 1962. Contains the MS
Venice, Bib. Marciana, MS Ital. iv. 1227 complete.

Jeppesen, Knud, *Die Italienische Orgelmusik am Anfang des Cinquecento*, 1–2; Hansen,
Copenhagen 1960 (2nd, enlarged ed.). Includes Marco Antonio Cavazzoni's
Recerchari, motetti, canҳoni, 1523, complete; six pieces from *Frottole intabulate
da sonare organi*, Antonio Gardani, Venice 1551; and eight pieces from the
Castell' Arquato MS.

Johannes of Lublin, *Tablature of Keyboard Music*, 1–6, ed. John R. White: *CEKM*, 6;
American Institute of Musicology, 1964–67. The largest Polish anthology of
early keyboard music. See also Facsimiles, above.

Kastner, Macário Santiago, *Silva Ibérica*, 1–2; Schott, Mainz 1954/65. 16th–18th-
century Spanish keyboard music. *Cravistas Portugueҳes*, 1–2; Schott, Mainz
1935/50. Early Portuguese keyboard music.

Marx, Hans Joachim, *Tabulaturen des 16. Jahrhundert*, 1–2: *Schweiҳerische Musik-
denkmäler*, 6 & 7; Bärenreiter, Basle 1967. The first volume contains Kotter's
two MSS complete, with two lesser MSS; the second, the Clemens Hör Tablature.

Melothesia, Keyboard Suites from, 1673, ed. Anthony Kooiker; Pennsylvania State
University Press, 1968. 32 selected pieces by Anon., John Banister, Gerhard
Diesner, William Gregory, William Hall, John Moss, Christopher Preston,
John Roberts, Robert Smith, and William Thatcher. The selection omits ten
further pieces by Anon., Gregory, and Preston, and all the pieces by Matthew
Locke (for whom, see Composers, below).

Merian, Wilhelm, *Der Tanҳ in den deutschen Tabulaturbüchern*; Breitkopf & Härtel,
Leipzig 1928. Reprinted by Olms, Hildesheim 1968. Includes 184 pieces from the
tablatures of Kotter, Ammerbach, Schmid the Elder and the Younger, Paix,
Löffelholtz, Nörmiger, and Mareschall.

Mulliner Book, The, ed. Denis Stevens: *Musica Britannica*, 1; Stainer & Bell, London
1951. *The Mulliner Book: a Commentary*, by the same author and publisher, is
issued separately.

Musicks Hand-maide, 1663, ed. Thurston Dart; Stainer & Bell, London 1970.

Musick's Hand-maid, The Second Part of, 1689, ed. Thurston Dart; Stainer & Bell,
London 1962 (2nd ed.).

Noske, Frits, *Klavierboek van Anna Maria van Eyl: Monumenta Musica Neerlandica*,
2; Vereniging voor Nederlandse Musiekgeschiedenis, Amsterdam 1959.

Oesterle, Louis, *Early Keyboard Music*, 1–2; Schirmer, New York 1932. A good
selection of pieces from Byrd to Scarlatti; but the texts are over-edited and often
unreliable.

Parthenia, 1612/13, ed. Thurston Dart; Stainer & Bell, London 1960. 21 pieces by
Byrd, Bull, & Gibbons: 'The first musicke that euer was printed for the virginalls'. See also Facsimiles, above.

Parthenia In-Violata, c. 1620–29, ed. Thurston Dart; Peters, New York 1961. 20 pieces for virginals and bass viol, the latter optional. See also Facsimiles, above.

Seiffert, Max, *Organum*, Reihe IV: *Orgelmusik*, 1–22; Reihe V: *Klaviermusik*, 1–10; Leipzig 1925–26.

Stevens, Denis, *Altenglische Orgelmusik*; Bärenreiter, Kassel 1954.

Tagliapietra, Gino, *Antologia de musica antica e moderna per pianoforte*, 1–18; Ricordi, Milan 1931–33. Second to Farrenc in comprehensiveness; but the texts are very over-edited and often unreliable.

Tisdale's Virginal Book, c. 1600, ed. Alan Brown; Stainer & Bell, London 1966.

Torchi, Luigi, *L'Arte musicale in Italia*, 1–7; Ricordi, Milan 1897–1907. The keyboard works are in Vol. 3.

Venegas de Henestrosa, Luis, *Libro de cifra nueva para tecla, arpa y vihuela*, 1557, ed. Higini Anglés: *Monumentos de la Musica Española*, 2 ('La musica en la corte de Carlos V'); Instituto Española de Musicologia, Barcelona 1965. The largest Spanish anthology of early keyboard music, including some 40 pieces by Antonio [de Cabezón].

COMPOSERS

AMMERBACH, ELIAS NICOLAUS c. 1530–97
see Anthologies, above, under Merian.

ARNE, THOMAS AUGUSTINE 1710–78
Eight Keyboard Sonatas (facsimile of 1st ed.), ed. G. Beechey & T. Dart; Stainer & Bell, London 1969.

BACH, CARL PHILIPP EMANUEL 1714–88
Sonaten, freien Fantasien und Rondos für Kenner und Liebhaber, 1–6, W. 55–59 & 61, ed. Carl Krebs; Breitkopf & Härtel, Leipzig 1895. Reprinted 1953.
[6] '*Württembergischen*' *Sonaten*, 1–2, W. 49, ed. Rudolf Steglich; Nagel, Hanover 1928.
[6] '*Preussischen*' *Sonaten*, 1–2, W. 48, ed. Rudolf Steglich; Nagel, Hanover 1928.
Sechs Sonaten (from *Versuch über die wahre Art das Clavier zu spielen*), 1–2, W. 63, ed. Erich Doflein; Schott, Mainz 1935.

BACH, JOHANN CHRISTIAN 1735–82
[10] *Sonaten*, ed. Ludwig Landshoff; Peters, Leipzig 1925.

BACH, JOHANN SEBASTIAN 1685–1750
Neue Bach-Ausgabe; Bärenreiter, Kassel 1954– . (In progress. 86 vols. planned, of which Series V will contain the Klavier works.)
Bachgesellschaft Ausgabe 1–46; Breitkopf & Härtel, Leipzig 1851–1900. Klavier works in vols. 3, 13/2, 14, 36, 42, and 45. Modern reprints, full size: Edwards, Ann Arbor; slightly reduced: Gregg, Farnborough; $5\frac{1}{2} \times 7$ ins: Lea Pocket Scores, New York.

Many separate eds., of which the following are specially useful:
Klavierwerke, 1–7, ed. Hans Bischoff; Steingräber, Leipzig 1880–88. Reprinted in part by Kalmus, New York. This was much the best 19th-century ed.
Inventionen und Sinfonien, ed. Ludwig Landshoff; Peters, Leipzig 1933. With an important separate *Revisionsbericht*.
Forty-Eight Preludes and Fugues, ed. Donald Francis Tovey; Associated Board, London 1924. Includes invaluable notes on each work.
The 'Goldberg' Variations, ed. Ralph Kirkpatrick; Schirmer, New York 1938. Includes an invaluable preface.
See also Facsimiles, above.

BACH, WILHELM FRIEDEMANN 1710–84
[*8*] *Fugen & [12] Polonaise*, ed. Walter Niemann; Peters, Leipzig 1914. Very over-edited.
[*9*] *Sonaten*, 1–3, ed. Friedrich Blume; Nagel, Kassel 1930/32/40.

BALBASTRE, CLAUDE 1729–99
Pièces de clavecin, ed. Alan Curtis; Heugel, Paris 1972.

BEETHOVEN, LUDWIG VAN 1770–1827
Werke, ed. under the auspices of the Beethoven-Archiv, Bonn; Henle, Munich 1961– . (In progress. Solo piano works in Abt. VIII.)
Werke, 1–32; Breitkopf & Härtel, Leipzig 1862–90. Solo piano works in vols. 20–23 and 32; piano duets in vol. 13. Modern reprints, full size: Edwards, Ann Arbor; 10×15 ins. & 5½×7 ins.: Kalmus, New York.
Many separate eds., of which the following are specially useful:
Sonatas, 1–3, ed. Donald Francis Tovey; Associated Board, London 1931. Includes invaluable notes on each work. *A Companion to Beethoven's Pianoforte Sonatas* by the same author and publisher is issued separately, and contains bar-by-bar analyses.
Klavierstücke, ed. Otto von Irmer; Henle, Munich 1950.
Sämtliche Bagatellen, ed. Otto von Irmer; Henle, Munich 1950.
Variationen für Klavier, 1–2, ed. Joseph Schmidt-Geörg; Henle, Munich 1961.
See also Facsimiles, above.

BLOW, JOHN 1647–1708
Six Suites, ed. Howard Ferguson; Stainer & Bell, London 1965.
30 Voluntaries and Verses for Organ, ed. Watkins Shaw; Schott, London 1972 (2nd ed.).
See also Anthologies, above, under Fuller Maitland.

BÖHM, GEORG 1661–1740
Sämtliche Werke für Klavier und Orgel, 1–2, ed. Johannes & Gesa Wolgast; Breitkopf & Härtel, Wiesbaden 1952. Vol. 1 contains the works for clavichord or harpsichord.

BOISMORTIER, JOSEPH BODIN DE 1691–1755
   4 Suites de pièces de clavecin, Op. 59, ed. Erwin R. Jacobi; Leuckart, Munich 1960.

BOUTMY, JOSSE 1697–1779
   Werken voor clavicimbel, ed. Joseph Watelet: *Monumenta Musica Belgicae*, 5; Berchem & Antwerp 1943.

BOYCE, WILLIAM c. 1710–79
   Ten Voluntaries for Organ or Harpsichord (facsimile of 1st ed.), ed. John Caldwell; Oxford Univ. Press 1972.

BRAHMS, JOHANNES 1833–97
   Sämtliche Werke, 1–26; Breitkopf & Härtel, Leipzig 1927–28. Solo piano works in vols. 13–15; piano duets in vol. 12. Paperback reprint of solo piano works in 3 vols. by Dover, New York.
   Many separate eds., of which the Henle, ed. Walter Georgii, is specially good.
   See also Facsimiles, above.

BRUHNS, NICOLAUS c. 1665–97
   Gesammelte Werke, 1–2, ed. Fritz Stein: *Das Erbe deutscher Musik*, Ser. II/1 & 2; Brunswick 1937/39.

BULL, JOHN c. 1563–1628
   Keyboard Music, 1–2, ed. J. Steele, F. Cameron, & T. Dart: *Musica Britannica*, 14 & 19; Stainer & Bell, London 1960/63.

BUXTEHUDE, DIDERIK 1637–1707
   Klaver Vaerker, ed. Emilius Bangert; Hansen, Copenhagen 1944. Contains the works for clavichord or harpsichord.
   Orgelcompositionen, 1–4, ed. Josef Hedar; Hansen, Copenhagen 1952. Also includes some harpsichord works.

BYRD, WILLIAM 1543–1623
   Keyboard Music, 1–2, ed. Alan Brown: *Musica Britannica*, 27 & 28; Stainer & Bell, London 1969/71.
   My Ladye Nevells Book, ed. Hilda Andrews; Curwen, London 1926. Paperback reprint by Dover, New York.

CABEZÓN, ANTONIO DE 1500–66
   Gesamtausgabe, ed. Charles Jacobs; Institute of Mediaeval Music, New York 1967–. (In progress.)
   Obras de música para tecla, arpa y vihuela, 1–3, ed. Higini Anglès: *Monumentos de la Música Española*, 27–29; Instituto Española de Musicologia, Barcelona 1966.
   See also Anthologies, above, under Venegas.

CAVAZZONI, GIROLAMO c. 1510–c. 1580
   Orgelwerke, 1–2, ed. Oscar Mischiati; Schott, Mainz 1959/61.

CAVAZZONI, MARCO ANTONIO c. 1490–c. 1570
   See Anthologies, above, under Jeppesen.

CHAMBONNIÈRES, JACQUES CHAMPION DE *c.* 1602–*c.* 1672
Œuvres complètes, ed. P. Brunold & A. Tessier; Senart, Paris 1925. Reprinted by
Broude, New York.
Pièces de clauessin, 1–2, 1670, ed. Thurston Dart; Oiseau-Lyre, Monaco 1970.
See also Facsimiles, above.

CHOPIN, FRÉDÉRIC 1810–49
Complete Works, 1–21, ed. under the auspices of The Fryderyk Chopin Institute,
Warsaw; Polskie Wydawnictwo Muzyczne, Warsaw 1949–62.
Many other eds., of which the Henle, ed. Ewald Zimmermann, is specially good,
though as yet incomplete.
See also Facsimiles, above.

CIMAROSA, DOMENICO 1749–1801
32 Sonatas, 1–3, ed. Felice Boghen; Paris 1925–26.

CLARKE, JEREMIAH *c.* 1673–1707
See Anthologies, above, under Fuller Maitland.

CLEMENTI, MUZIO 1746–1832
No complete ed. at present available. Various publishers issue different selections.

CLÉRAMBAULT, LOUIS NICOLAS 1676–1749
Pièces de clavecin, ed. P. Brunold & T. Dart; Oiseau-Lyre, Monaco 1964.
See also Anthologies, under Guilmant.

COELHO, MANUEL RODRIGUES *b.* 1583
Flores de musica, 1–2, ed. Macário Santiago Kastner: *Portugaliae Musica*, 1 & 3;
Gulbenkian, Lisbon 1959/61.

CORNET, PETER ?–?
Collected Keyboard Works, ed. Willi Apel: *CEKM*, 27; American Institute of Musicology, 1969.

CORREA DE ARAUXO, FRANCISCO *c.* 1576–1653
Libro de tientos, 1–2, ed. Macário Santiago Kastner: *Monumentos de la Música
Española*, 6 and 12; Instituto Española de Musicologia, Barcelona 1948/52.

COUPERIN, FRANÇOIS 1669–1733
Pièces de clavecin, 1–4, ed. Kenneth Gilbert; Heugel, Paris 1969–72. This ed. is
more reliable than any other.
L'Art de toucher le clavecin, ed. in French, German, & English by Anna Linde;
Breitkopf & Härtel, Leipzig 1933.
See also Facsimiles, above.

COUPERIN, LOUIS *c.* 1626–62
Pièces de clavecin, ed. P. Brunold & T. Dart; Oiseau-Lyre, Monaco 1959.
Pièces de clavecin, ed. Alan Curtis; Heugel, Paris 1970. Based on the recently
discovered 'Parville MS'.
Neither of these eds. is wholly complete, so both are required.

CROFT, WILLIAM 1678–1727
Complete Harpsichord Works, 1–2, ed. H. Ferguson & C. Hogwood; Stainer & Bell, London 1974.
See also Anthologies, under Fuller Maitland.

DAGINCOUR, FRANÇOIS *c.* 1684–1758
Pièces de clavecin, ed. Howard Ferguson; Heugel, Paris 1969.
Pièces d'orgue, ed. Ludovic Panel; Schola Cantorum, Paris 1956.

DANDRIEU, JEAN FRANÇOIS 1682–1738
3 Livres de Clavecin, ed. P. Aubert & B. François-Sappey; Schola Cantorum, Paris 1973.

D'ANGLEBERT, JEAN HENRY 1635–91
Pièces de clavecin, ed. Marguerete Rœsgen-Champion; Société Française de Musicologie, Paris 1934.
See also Facsimiles, above.

DAQUIN, LOUIS CLAUDE 1694–1772
Pièces de clavecin, ed. Paul Brunold; Senart, Paris 19—.

DIEUPART, CHARLES *d. c.* 1740
Six Suites, ed. Paul Brunold; Oiseau-Lyre, Paris 1934.

DUPHLY, JACQUES 1715–89
Pièces pour le clavecin, ed. Françoise Petit; Heugel, Paris 1967.

DURANTE, FRANCESCO 1684–1755
Studii, divertimenti e toccate, ed. Bernhard Paumgartner; Bärenreiter, Kassel 1949.

ECKHARD, JOHANN GOTTFRIED *c.* 1735–1809
Klavierwerke, ed. Eduard Reeser; Bärenreiter, Kassel 1956.

ERBACH, CHRISTIAN 1573–1635
Collected Keyboard Compositions, ed. Clare G. Rayner: *CEKM*, 36; American Institute of Musicology, 1971.

FACOLI, MARCO ?–?
Intavolatura di balli, 1588, ed. Willi Apel: *CEKM*, 2; American Institute of Musicology, 1963.

FARNABY, GILES (*c.* 1566–1640) and RICHARD (*b. c.* 1590)
Keyboard Music, ed. Richard Marlow: *Musica Britannica*, 24; Stainer & Bell, London 1965.

FIELD, JOHN 1782–1837
18 Nocturnes, ed. Louis Koehler; Peters, Leipzig [n.d.]. Very over-edited.

FIOCCO, JOSEPH HECTOR 1703–41
Werken voor Clavicimbel, ed. Joseph Watelet: *Monumenta Musica Belgicae*, 3; Berchem & Antwerp 1936.

FISCHER, JOHANN KASPAR FERDINAND *c.* 1665–1746
Sämtliche Werke für Klavier und Orgel, ed. Ernst von Werra; Breitkopf & Härtel, Leipzig 1901. Reprinted by Broude, New York.

FORQUERAY, ANTOINE *c.* 1671–1745
Pièces de clavecin, ed. Colin Tilney; Heugel, Paris 1970.

FRESCOBALDI, GIROLAMO 1583–1643
Orgel- und Klavierwerke, 1–5, ed. Pierre Pidoux; Bärenreiter, Kassel 1948/49.
Containing most of the works published during the composer's lifetime.
Keyboard Compositions at Present in MSS, 1–3, ed. W. R. Shindle: *CEKM,* 30;
American Institute of Musicology, 1968.

FROBERGER, JOHANN JAKOB 1616–67
Orgel und Klavierwerke, 1–3, ed. Guido Adler: *Denkmäler der Tonkunst in Oester-
reich,* 8, 13, & 21; Artaria, Vienna 1897/99 & 1903. Reprinted by Akademische
Druck- und Verlagsanstalt, Graz 1959.

FUX, JOHANN JOSEPH 1660–1741
Werke für Tasteninstrumente, ed. Erich Schenk: *Denkmäler der Tonkunst in Oesterreich,* 85; Vienna 1947.

GABRIELI, ANDREA *c.* 1520–86
Orgelwerke, 1–5, ed. Pierre Pidoux; Bärenreiter, Kassel 1952.

GABRIELI, GIOVANNI 1557–1612
Composizioni per organo, 1–3, ed. Sandro Dalla Libera; Ricordi, Milan 1957/59.

GALUPPI, BALDASSARE 1706–85
Dodici sonate, ed. G. Benvenuti; Pizzi, Bologna 1920.
Six Sonatas, ed. Edith Woodcock; Galliard, London 1963.
Passatempo al cembalo: [*6*] *sonate,* ed. Franco Piva; Istituto per la Collaborazione
culturale, Venice 1964.

GIBBONS, CHRISTOPHER 1615–76
Keyboard Compositions, ed. Clare G. Rayner: *CEKM,* 18; American Institute of
Musicology, 1967.

GIBBONS, ORLANDO 1583–1625
Keyboard Music, ed. Gerald Hendrie: *Musica Britannica,* 20; Stainer & Bell, London
1962.

GIUSTINI, LUDOVICO ?–?
See Facsimiles, above.

GRAUPNER, JOHANN CHRISTOPH 1683–1760
Drei Partien, ed. Albert Küster; Wolfenbüttel 1935.
8 Partien, ed. Lothar Hoffman-Erbrecht: *Mitteldeutsches Musik-Archiv,* Ser. 1/2;
Leipzig 1954.
Monatliche Klavier-Früchte, ed. Albert Küster; Wolfenbüttel 1928–29.

GRAZIOLI, GIOVANNI BATTISTA *c.* 1750–*c.* 1820
Dodici sonate per cembalo, ed. Ruggiero Gerlin: *I classici musicali italiani,* 12;
Milan 1943.

GRIEG, EDVARD 1843–1907
Complete Piano Works, 1–3; Peters, Leipzig [n.d.].

HANDEL, GEORGE FRIDERIC 1685–1759
Klavierwerke, 1–3, ed. R. Steglich, P. Northway, & T. Best; Bärenreiter, Kassel 1955/70.
Pieces for Harpsichord, 1–2 [the Aylesford MSS], ed. W. Barclay Squire & J. A. Fuller Maitland; Schott, London 1928.

HASSE, JOHANN ADOLF 1699–1783
Claviersonaten, ed. Richard Engländer; Leipzig 1930.

HASSLER, HANS LEO 1564–1612
Werke für Orgel und Klavier, ed. Adolf Sandberger: *Denkmäler der Tonkunst in Bayern*, 4/2; Breitkopf & Härtel, Leipzig 1903. Reprinted 1968.

HAVINGHA, GERHARDUS 1696–1753
Werken voor Clavicimbel, ed. Joseph Watelet: *Monumenta musica Belgicae*, 7; Berchem & Antwerp 1951.

HAYDN, JOSEPH 1732–1809
Werke, ed. under the auspices of the Joseph Haydn-Institute, Cologne; Henle, Munich 1960– . (In progress. The Piano Sonatas, 1–3, ed. Georg Feder, are in Reihe XVIII.)
Sämtliche Klaviersonaten, 1–3, ed. Christa Landon; Universal, Vienna 1964.
Klavierstücke, ed. Kurt Soldan; Peters, Frankfurt 1956.
Flötenuhrstücke, ed. Ernst Fritz Schmid; Nagel, Hanover 1931. Thirty-two pieces for mechanical clock.

HELMONT, CHARLES JOSEPH VAN 1715–90
Werken voor Orgel en Clavicimbel, ed. Joseph Watelet: *Monumenta Musica Belgicae*, 6; Berchem & Antwerp 1948.

HURLEBUSCH, CONRAD FRIEDRICH 1696–1765
Compositioni musicali per il cembalo, ed. Max Seiffert: *Monumenta Musica Neerlandica*, 32; Vereniging voor Nederlandse Musiekgeschiedenis, Amsterdam 1912.

ILEBORGH, ADAM ?–?
See Facsimiles, above; also Anthologies, above, under Apel.

JACQUET DE LA GUERRE, ELIZABETH c. 1664–1729
Pièces de clavecin, ed. P. Brunold & T. Dart; Oiseau-Lyre, Monaco 1965.

KERLL, JOHANN KASPAR 1627–93
Ausgewählte Werke, 1, ed. Adolf Sandberger: *Denkmäler der Tonkunst in Bayern*, 2/2; Breitkopf & Härtel, Leipzig 1901. Reprinted 1968.

KINDERMANN, JOHANN ERASMUS 1616–55
Ausgewählte Werke, 1–2, ed. F. Schreiber & B. A. Wallner: *Denkmäler der Tonkunst in Bayern*, 21 & 24; Breitkopf & Härtel, Leipzig 1913. Reprinted 1968.

KOTTER, HANS *c.* 1485–1541
See Anthologies, above, under Marx and Merian.

KREBS, JOHANN LUDWIG 1712–80
Klavierübung, ed. Kurt Soldan; Peters, Leipzig 1937.

KRIEGER, JOHANN 1651–1735
Gesammelte Werke für Klavier und Orgel, ed. Max Seiffert: *Denkmäler der Tonkunst in Bayern*, 30; Breitkopf & Härtel, Leipzig 1917. Reprinted 1968.

KUHNAU, JOHANN 1660–1722
Klavierwerke, ed. Carl Päsler: *Denkmäler deutscher Tonkunst*, 4; Breitkopf & Härtel, Leipzig 1901. Reprinted 1958.

LEBÈGUE, NICOLAS 1631–1702
Œuvres de clavecin, ed. Norbert Dufourcq; Oiseau-Lyre, Monaco 1956.

LE ROUX, GASPARD *c.* 1660–1707
Pieces for Harpsichord, ed. Albert Fuller; Alpeg, New York 1959.

LISZT, FRANZ 1811–86
Complete Works; Bärenreiter, Kassel 1970– . (In progress. The works for solo piano are in Series I.)
Gesammelte Werke, 1–34, ed. under the auspices of the Franz Liszt Stiftung; Breitkopf & Härtel, Leipzig 1901–36. (The works for solo piano, not quite complete, are in Series II.) Reprint, slightly reduced size: Gregg, Farnborough 1966.
Liszt Society Publications, 1–5; Schott, London [n.d.]. These vols. contain some of the lesser known works.

LOCKE, MATTHEW *c.* 1630–77
Keyboard Suites and *Organ Voluntaries*, ed. Thurston Dart; Stainer & Bell, London 1959/57. These two vols. contain the complete keyboard works.
See also Facsimiles, above.

LOEILLET, JEAN BAPTISTE 1680–1730
Werken voor Clavicimbel, ed. Joseph Watelet: *Monumenta Musica Belgicae*, 1; Berchem & Antwerp 1932.

LÖFFELHOLTZ, CHRISTHOF 16th century
See Anthologies, above, under Merian.

LÜBECK, VINCENT 1654–1740
Clavierübung, ed. H. Trede; Peters, Leipzig [1950].

LUBLIN, JOHANNES OF
See Facsimiles & Anthologies, above, under Johannes.

MARCELLO, BENEDETTO 1686–1739
[12] *Sonates pour le clavecin*, ed. L. Sgrizzi & L. Bianconi; Heugel, Paris 1971.

MARCHAND, LOUIS 1667–1723
Pièces de clavecin, ed. Thurston Dart; Oiseau-Lyre, Monaco 1960.

MARESCHALL, SAMUEL 1554–1640

Selected Works, ed. Jean-Marie Bonhote: *CEKM*, 27; American Institute of Musicology, 1967.

See also Anthologies, above, under Merian.

MARTINI, GIOVANNI BATTISTA 1706–84

Dodici sonate per cembalo od organo, ed. M. Vitali; Milan [n.d.].

MATTHESON, JOHANN 1618–1764

Die wohlklingende Fingersprache, ed. Lothar Hoffman-Erbrecht: *Mitteldeutsches Musik-Archiv*, Ser. 1/1; Leipzig 1954.

See also Facsimiles, above.

MENDELSSOHN, FELIX 1809–47

Werke, 1–23, ed. Julius Rietz; Breitkopf & Härtel, Leipzig 1874–77. (The works for piano solo are in Ser. 11; piano duets in Ser. 10.) Reprint, slightly reduced size: Gregg, Farnborough 1967–68.

MERULA, TARQUINIO ?–?

Composizione per organo e cimbalo, ed. Alan Curtis: *Monumenti de musica italiani*, 1; Brescia 1961.

MERULO, CLAUDIO 1533–1604

Toccate, 1–3, ed. Sandro Dalla Libera; Ricordi, Milan 1959.

Canzonen, 1592, ed. Pierre Pidoux; Bärenreiter, Kassel 1954.

MONDONVILLE, JEAN-JOSEPH CASSANÉA DE 1711–72

Pièces de clavecin en sonate, 1, ed. Marc Pincherle: *Société française de musicologie*, 9; Paris 1935.

MORLEY, THOMAS 1557–c. 1602

Keyboard Works, 1–2, ed. Thurston Dart; Stainer & Bell, London 1959.

MOZART, WOLFGANG AMADEUS 1756–91

Neue Ausgabe sämtlicher Werke, ed. under the auspices of the Internationale Stiftung Mozarteum, Salzburg; Bärenreiter, Kassel 1955– . (In progress. Works for solo piano and duet in Ser. 9.)

Werke, 1–74; Breitkopf & Härtel, Leipzig 1887–1905. (Works for piano solo in vols 20 & 21; for piano duet in vol. 19. Reprinted by Edwards, Ann Arbor.)

Sonatas for Pianoforte, ed. S. Sadie & D. Matthews; Associated Board, London 1970– . (In progress.)

Klavierstücke, ed. Bertha Antonia Wallner; Henle, Munich 1955.

Variationen, ed. Ewald Zimmermann; Henle, Munich 1959.

See also Facsimiles, above.

MUFFAT, GEORG 1653–1704

Apparatus Musico-Organisticus, 1690, ed. R. Walter; Coppenrath, Altötting 1957.

MUFFAT, GOTTLIEB THEOPHILIUS 1690–1770

Componimenti musicali, ed. Guido Adler: *Denkmäler der Tonkunst in Oesterreich*, 7; Artaria, Vienna 1896. Reprinted Graz 1959.

See also Facsimiles, above.

MURSCHHAUSER, FRANZ XAVER ANTON 1663–1738
Gesammelte Werke für Klavier und Orgel, ed. Max Seiffert: *Denkmäler der Tonkunst in Bayern,* 18; Breitkopf & Härtel, Leipzig 1917.

NOORDT, ANTHONI VAN *d. c.* 1675
Tabulatuur-Boek, ed. Max Seiffert, revised P. Lagas: *Monumenta Musica Neerlandica,* 19; Vereniging voor Nederlandse Musiekgeschiedenis, Amsterdam 1912.

NÖRMIGER, AUGUST 16th century
See Anthologies, above, under Merian.

PACHELBEL, JOHANN 1653–1706
Klavierwerke, ed. Adolf Sandberger: *Denkmäler der Tonkunst in Bayern,* 2; Breitkopf & Härtel, Leipzig 1901. Reprinted in 1968.
Hexachordium Apollinis, 1699, ed. Hans Joachim Moser & Traugott Fedke; Bärenreiter, Kassel 1964.

PACHELBEL, WILHELM HIERONYMUS 1685–1764
Werke für Orgel und Clavier, ed. H. J. Moser & T. Fedke; Bärenreiter, Kassel 1957.

PAIX, JACOB 1550–*c.* 1617
See Anthologies, above, under Merian.

PARADIES, PIETRO DOMENICO 1707–91
[*12*] *Sonate per pianoforte,* ed. Dante Cipollini; Notari, Milan 1920.

PASQUINI, BERNARDO 1637–1710
Collected Works for Keyboard, 1–7, ed. Maurice Brooks Haynes: *CEKM,* 5; American Institute of Musicology, 1964–68.

PASQUINI, ERCOLE ?–?
Collected Keyboard Works, ed. W. R. Shindle: *CEKM,* 12; American Institute of Musicology, 1966.

PAUMANN, CONRAD *c.* 1410–73
See Anthologies, above, under Apel.

PESCETTI, GIOVANNI BATTISTA *c.* 1704–*c.* 1766
Sonates, ed. L. Bianconi & L. Sgrizzi; Heugel, Paris 1972.

PICCHI, GIOVANNI ?–?
See under Facsimiles, above.

POGLIETTI, ALESSANDRO *d.* 1683
The 'Rossignolo' suite and some other pieces are published in *Denkmäler der Tonkunst in Oesterreich,* 27; Artaria, Vienna 1906. Reprinted Akademische Druck- und Verlagsanstalt, Graz 1959.

PURCELL, DANIEL *c.* 1660–1717
See Anthologies, above, under Fuller Maitland.

PURCELL, HENRY *c.* 1659–95
Eight Suites and *Miscellaneous Keyboard Pieces,* ed. Howard Ferguson; Stainer & Bell, London 1968 (2nd ed.). The two vols. comprise the complete harpsichord works.

Organ Works, ed. Hugh McLean; Novello, London 1957.
See also Facsimiles, above.

RADINO, GIOVANNI MARIA ?–?

Il primo libro d'intavolatura di balli d'arpicordi, 1592, ed. S. Ellingworth: *CEKM*,
33; American Institute of Musicology, 1968.
See also Facsimiles, above.

RAICK, DIEUDONNÉ DE *c.* 1702–64

Werken voor Clavicimbel, ed. Joseph Watelet: *Monumenta Musica Belgicae*, 6;
Berchem & Antwerp 1948.

RAMEAU, JEAN-PHILIPPE 1683–1764

Pièces de clavecin, ed. Erwin R. Jacobi; Bärenreiter, Kassel 1958.
See also Facsimiles, above.

REDFORD, JOHN *d.* 1547

Keyboard works, in the appendix of C. F. Pfatteicher, *John Redford*; Bärenreiter,
Kassel 1934.
See also Anthologies, above, under *Tudor Organ Music*, 1–2.

REINKEN, ADAM 1623–1722

Collected Keyboard Works, ed. Willi Apel: *CEKM*, 16; American Institute of Musicology, 1967.

ROGERS, BENJAMIN 1614–98

Complete Harpsichord Works, ed. Richard Rastall; Stainer & Bell, London 1972.

ROSEINGRAVE, THOMAS 1690–1766

Compositions for Organ & Harpsichord, ed. Denis Stevens; Pennsylvania State
Univ. Press, 1964. A selection containing four suites, etc.
See also Facsimiles, above.

ROSSI, MICHELANGELO *c.* 1600–*c.* 1660

Collected Keyboard Works, ed. John R. White: *CEKM*, 15; American Institute of
Musicology, 1966.

SALVATORE, GIOVANNI *d. c.* 1688

Collected Keyboard Works, ed. B. Hudson: *CEKM*, 3; American Institute of Musicology, 1964.

SCARLATTI, ALESSANDRO 1660–1726

Primo e secondo libro di toccate, ed. Ruggiero Gerlin: *I classici musicali italiani*, 13;
Milan 1943.
[*29*] *Toccate per cembalo*, ed. J. S. Shedlock; Bach, London 1908–10. (From the
'Higgs' MS.)

SCARLATTI, DOMENICO 1685–1757

[*555*] *Sonates*, 1–11, ed. Kenneth Gilbert; Heugel, Paris 1971– . (In progress.
The only reliable complete ed.)

Sixty Sonatas, 1–2, ed. Ralph Kirkpatrick; Schirmer, New York 1953. Includes an invaluable preface.

See also Facsimiles, above.

SCHEIDT, SAMUEL 1587–1654

Werke, 1–7, ed. Christhard Marenholz; Ugrino, Hamburg 1953. The keyboard works are in Vols. 6 & 7.

SCHLICK, ARNOLT *c.* 1455–*c.* 1525

Tabulaturen etlicher Lobgesang und Lidlein, 1512, ed. Gottfried Harms; Ugrino, Hamburg 1957.

SCHMID, BERNHART THE ELDER (1520–*c.* 1592), and THE YOUNGER (*b.* 1548)

See Anthologies, above, under Merian; also Facsimiles, above.

SCHUBERT, FRANZ 1797–1828

Neue Ausgabe sämtlicher Werke; Bärenreiter, Kassel 1964– . (In progress. Series VII will contain the piano solo and duet works.)

Gesammelte Werke, 1–41; Breitkopf & Härtel, Leipzig 1884–97. (Works for piano solo in Ser. 10–12, & 21; piano duets in Ser. 9.) Reprinted, slightly reduced size, by Dover, New York 1965, with the works for piano solo in vols 5 & 18, and the piano duets in vol. 4. Dover also issue the *Piano Sonatas* and *Shorter Works for Piano Solo* as two paperbacks (excluding the Dances).

Sonatas for Piano, ed. Howard Ferguson; Associated Board, London 197– . This new ed., including the unfinished sonatas, is in preparation.

See also Facsimiles, above.

SCHUMANN, ROBERT 1810–56

Gesammelte Werke, 1–32; Breitkopf & Härtel, Leipzig 1881–93. (Works for piano solo in Ser. 7; piano duets in Ser. 6.) Reprinted, reduced size, by Gregg, Farnborough 1967–68.

See also Facsimiles above.

SEIXAS, CARLOS 1704–42

80 Sonatas, ed. Macário Santiago Kastner: *Portugaliae Musica*, 10; Gulbenkian, Lisbon 1965.

SOLER, ANTONIO 1729–83

Sonatas para instrumentos de tecla, 1–6, ed. P. S. Rubio; Union Musical Español, Madrid 1957–62.

STEIGLEDER, JOHANN ULRICH 1593–1635

Compositions for Keyboard, 1–2, ed. Willi Apel: *CEKM*, 13; American Institute of Musicology, 1968–69.

STORACE, BERNARDO ?–?

Selva di varie compositioni d'intavolatura per cimbalo ed organo, 1644, ed. Barton Hudson: *CEKM*, 7; American Institute of Musicology, 1965.

STROZZI, GREGORIO ?–?
Capricci da sonare cembali et organi, 1687, ed. Barton Hudson: *CEKM*, 11; American Institute of Musicology, 1967.

SWEELINCK, JAN PIETERSZOON 1562–1621
Opera Omnia, 1: *Keyboard Works*, fasc. 1–3, ed. G. Leonhardt, A. Annegarn, & F. Noske; Vereniging voor Nederlandse Musiekgeschiedenis, Amsterdam 1968.

TALLIS, THOMAS *c.* 1505–1585
Complete Keyboard Works, ed. Denis Stevens; Hinrichsen, London 1953.

TELEMANN, GEORG PHILIPP 1681–1767
[6] Fugues légères et petits jeux, c. 1730, ed. Martin Lange; Bärenreiter, Kassel 1929.
XX kleine Fugen, 1731, in *Orgelwerke*, 2, ed. Traugott Fedke; Bärenreiter, Kassel 1964.
[36] Fantaisies pour le clavecin, c. 1740, ed. Max Seiffert; Bärenreiter, Kassel 1935. Reprinted by Broude, New York.
VI Ouvertüren, c. 1745, ed. Hugo Ruf; Schott, Mainz 1967.

TISDALL, WILLIAM ?–?
Complete Keyboard Works, ed. Howard Ferguson; Stainer & Bell, London 1970 (2nd ed.).

TOMKINS, THOMAS 1572–1656
Keyboard Music, ed. Stephen Tuttle: *Musica Britannica*, 5; Stainer & Bell, London 1955.

VALENTE, ANTONIO ?–?
Intavolatura de Cimbalo, 1576, ed. Charles Jacobs; Clarendon Press, Oxford 1973.

WEBER, CARL MARIA VON 1786–1826
Sämtliche Werke [for piano], 1–3, ed. L. Köhler & A. Ruthardt; Peters, Leipzig [n.d.].

WECKMANN, MATTIAS 1619–74
Gesammelte Werke, ed. Gerhard Ilgner: *Das Erbe deutscher Musik*, Ser. 2/4; Brunswick 1942.

WEELKES, THOMAS *d.* 1623
Pieces for Keyed Instruments, ed. Margaret H. Glyn; Stainer & Bell, London 1924.

ZACHAU, FRIEDRICH WILHELM 1663–1712
Gesammelte Werke, 1–2, ed. Max Seiffert: *Denkmäler deutscher Tonkunst*, 21 & 22; Breitkopf & Härtel, Leipzig 1905. Reprinted 1958.

ZIPOLI, DOMENICO 1688–1726
Orgel- und Cembalowerke, 1–2, ed. Luigi Fernando Tagliavini; Müller, Heidelberg 1959. The harpsichord works are in vol. 2.

Index